THE barcelona COOKBOOK

THE
barcelona
COOKBOOK

a celebration of food, wine, and life

Sasa Mahr-Batuz and Andy Pforzheimer
with Mary Goodbody

Photography by John Blais

Andrews McMeel
Publishing, LLC
Kansas City

09 10 11 12 13 SDB 10 9 8 7 6 5 4 3 2 1

LIBRARY OF CONGRESS CATALOGING-IN-PUBLICATION DATA

Mahr-Batuz, Sasa.
 The Barcelona cookbook : a celebration of food, wine, and life / by Sasa Mahr-Batuz and Andy Pforzheimer with Mary Goodbody ; photography by John Blais.—1st ed.
   p. cm.
 Includes index.
 ISBN-13: 978-0-7407-7394-5
 ISBN-10: 0-7407-7394-1
 1. Cookery, Spanish. 2. Cookery, Mediterranean. 3. Tapas. 4. Barcelona Restaurant and Wine Bar. I. Pforzheimer, Andy. II. Goodbody, Mary. III. Barcelona Restaurant and Wine Bar. IV. Title.

 TX723.5.S7M2865 2009
 641.5946—dc22

                          2008032696

Design: Diane Marsh
Food Styling: Jennifer Prichett

Photos courtesy of Sasa Mahr-Batuz: i, v, x, xiv bottom, xv, xvi bottom, xvii, xviii right, xix, xx, xxii top right, 1, 9, 11, 12, 13, 14, 20, 21, 26 left and top right, 32, 34, 38, 39, 40–41, 43, 44, 49, 50, 59, 60, 61, 63, 65, 68–69, 70, 72 top, 81, 83, 98, 100, 105, 106, 111, 116, 117, 123, 127, 129, 132 right, 134 top right and left, 136, 139, 140, 155 right, 159 left, 161, 166, 171, 196

Photos by Felipe Rodríguez: 84–85, 102–103

www.andrewsmcmeel.com

www.barcelonawinebar.com

attention: schools and businesses

Andrews McMeel books are available at quantity discounts with bulk purchase for educational, business, or sales promotional use. For information, please write to: Special Sales Department, Andrews McMeel Publishing, LLC, 1130 Walnut Street, Kansas City, Missouri 64106.

To Zaneta and Zelie, and to all the talented,
hardworking people at Barcelona

contents

acknowledgments

This book would not be possible without the genius and creativity of chefs both past and present: Martha Hartley, Bill Rosenberg, Dave Curtis, Jose Palacios, Pedro Garzon, Elder Morales, Antonio Saldana, and Victor Sanchez all have invented and perfected the dishes that appear on these pages. Pedro and Adam Halberg have shaped the menus for the company as a whole, and Lisa Varnberg, in addition to creating some Barcelona classics, spent countless hours testing and transcribing recipes that were little more than scribbled notes on crumpled paper when she got them. Gretchen Thomas poured her encyclopedic knowledge of wine onto these pages. Mary Goodbody worked day and night to turn our thoughts into words and even spent time shivering in fish coolers and butchering steaks. Jean Lucas, Kirsty Melville, and Tim Lynch at Andrews McMeel believed in Barcelona and in us enough to see this book through from beginning to end, and Jane Dystel, our inimitable agent, made the whole thing happen. We are deeply indebted to them for handling the hard part so that we could continue making tapas, pouring wine, and serving tables.

foreword by gerry dawes

Over the past five years, tapas bars have become increasingly popular, along with their steady stream of small plates such as grilled mushrooms, *patatas bravas*, *gambas al ajillo*, *jamón Ibérico*, *croquetas*, stuffed *piquillo* peppers, and hundreds of other small-portion Spanish—and not-so-Spanish—dishes.

Yankee Connecticut might be the last place you'd expect a tapas bar and restaurant to be successful, but Andy Pforzheimer and his business partner, Sasa Mahr-Batuz, have proved that tasty, quickly prepared Spanish-inspired food, a wonderful wine list, and the lively, informal ambience for which tapas bars are famous can be a hit anywhere. They began their Barcelona Restaurant and Wine Bar concept several years ago with a single modest place across from a new movie theater in a then-gentrifying commercial section of South Norwalk (SoNo). The original Barcelona boomed, expanded into a full restaurant in its SoNo locale, and has since grown into a chain of five. Andy and Sasa are obviously bullish about tapas; they are preparing to open a sixth location in Stamford.

Tapas are going mainstream, and are heading toward the same general acceptance as pizza and sushi. And Barcelona will be a major player in making tapas as "American" as pizza, sushi, and, who knows, apple pie. For me, a forty-year veteran of gastronomic and wine travel in Spain, driving an hour from my home in the Hudson River valley to one of the Barcelona Restaurant and Wine Bars to enjoy a meal from the Spanish-inspired tapas menu and a good bottle of wine from the well-chosen list is the next best thing to being in Spain.

What Is Barcelona?

The lights are dim, the music is loud but not overpowering, the conversation is punctuated with laughter. Most of all, the heady aromas emanating from the kitchen—an intoxicating blend of garlic, grilled meats, shellfish, wine, and paprika—excite the senses. This is going to be a great evening! Look around. The walls are covered with bold art, the tables are topped with flickering candles and white cloths, the floor is polished tile and wood. You might have been transported to a fashionable eatery somewhere along the Mediterranean coast . . . to believe it, all you have to do is close your eyes and breathe it all in.

Welcome to the world of Barcelona Restaurant and Wine Bars. None of the six establishments is in Europe; all are in Connecticut, the New England state where Mark Twain lived and wrote. Nothing about any of our wine bars and restaurants has much to do with Connecticut Yankees if you discount the fresh food grown lovingly on local farms. Instead, we are dedicated to the easy, good food and dining attitudes of Spain—with

some very positive nods to the cooking of the United States and a few other countries. We search for the best ingredients at the local markets and from nearby farms. We also rely on imported Spanish spices, olive oils, vinegars, cheeses, olives, and cured meats. All of this bounty is used in dishes that are cooked simply so that the flavors burst into life.

For years now we have been entertaining people at our wine and tapas bars. Our guests know there will be laughter, great conversation, and terrific food and drink. By the end of every evening, they go home well fed, well cared for, and happy. Since not everyone can find his or her way to Connecticut, we decided to bring our food and our perception of good times to you, with *The Barcelona Cookbook*. Here you will find dozens of recipes for cold and hot tapas as well as a number of main courses, side dishes, and desserts guaranteed to make any meal shine. We also have menus for tapas parties and for an *asado*—an Argentine barbecue sure to be a major hit at your next party. But first, you might wonder exactly who we are. Before we continue, let us introduce ourselves.

who we are

We are Sasa Mahr-Batuz and Andy Pforzheimer, two guys with a dream, some luck, and an idea that worked. We opened our first restaurant in 1996 and very early on confronted the question "What is authentically Spanish?" We chose the name Barcelona because, while we planned to offer an authentic tapas experience, we wanted to feature a wide-ranging selection of Mediterranean food and wine. Spain's Barcelona is a cosmopolitan, pan-European city that reflects this outlook.

We did not meet each other until we decided to start a business together. Sasa wanted to open a tapas bar, and Andy, who is a trained chef, was solidly behind the idea. We both like restaurants and thrive on their hectic, frenetic pace. When we opened, we found a location in South Norwalk, an industrial-style downtown area called SoNo, in affluent Fairfield county. It was an ideal fit with our food, our wine, and our attitude—which is a little edgy with a big welcome. Norwalk is about 50 miles east of New York City on the coast of the Long Island Sound. The commuter

train to and from Grand Central Station rumbles by a block from our front door, and so we knew our customers would be urbane diners, used to eating in some of the best restaurants in New York and around the world. Since then, we have opened six more Barcelonas and learned a lot along the way.

This is our story and the food and drink we are passionate about.

sasa's story

There is something very special about sitting around a fire into the late hours of the night, socializing with good friends and grilling delicious foods. In fact, I can't think of a better way to spend time with the people you love.

I come by this appreciation honestly. When I was a boy, my family lived in Argentina, where life is a simple affair celebrated nearly every evening with friends, good wine, and great *asados*—the grilled meats Argentineans so love. Everywhere in the capital city of Buenos Aires you can smell the tantalizing aroma of meat sizzling over a charcoal fire. You will find *asados* being cooked in fine restaurants as well as by street vendors. People without backyards set up cinder blocks on the sidewalks, balance a grate on them, and build a fire to cook the meat. It's not uncommon to find groups of happy Argentineans sitting around one of these makeshift braziers long into the night. This gleeful approach to food imbued me with a love for the ritual surrounding mealtimes.

As far back as I can remember, food has been a big part of my life. Both of my parents loved to cook, and we four kids grew up helping in the kitchen. The great thing about learning to cook this way was that we laughed and joked while we worked together. In many ways, dinnertime was just one big party that we threw nearly every night.

My mother was born in Vienna, Austria, famous, of course, for its pastries, its Wiener schnitzel, and a delicious dumpling called a *knoedel* that is served with a wild mushroom sauce. She also had spent four years of her youth in Lago di Garda, Italy, where she embraced the cuisine with a passion, along with the culture and the language. I love her for that because it nurtured my own appreciation for Italian food.

My father came from Budapest, which has a long and proud culinary tradition. Among other things, it involves lots of paprika—think goulash and chicken paprikash—as well as delicacies such as spicy smoked *kolbasz* sausage; *töportyü*, a fatty bacon; and glorious Hungarian stuffed peppers.

My parents and their families left Europe during the Second World War and settled in Argentina, where they met, fell in love, and married and where three of their four children were born. There are vital English and Italian populations in Argentina, which have had a noticeable influence on the food. This meant that in addition to my parents' backgrounds, I was exposed to the cooking and food from a number of cultures—an exposure that was only enhanced when we later moved to Austria, where I learned to speak German and to enjoy the food and culture.

In 1973 my parents moved our family again, this time to New York City, where my father, a painter of modern art, secured his reputation and his fourth child was born. We were all profoundly affected by the experience. There was excitement in the air, a palpable sense that anything could happen.

During these years I developed a passion for tennis and eventually dropped out of high school to play full-time. I spent the next seven years traveling the world. My first overseas tournament was in Murcia, Spain. I fell in love with the country and with a beautiful girl, María Antonía García Jiménez, which explains why I played so often in Spain during those years. When, at the ripe old age of twenty-three, I realized I would not rise to the top of my sport, I decided to investigate other ways to make a living. I happened to be in Porto, Portugal, where I had just won both the singles and doubles open titles. The victories gave me a great deal of recognition around town, and, because I had good friends there as well, I decided to make the beautiful old city my home. I helped a friend open a successful aerobics and fitness center, while planning a pizza and fresh pasta store.

After a while I found my way back to the United States and got a job at a fabulous restaurant called Pasta Nostra in South Norwalk, Connecticut, where I learned a lot and met Carl Zuanelli, with whom I founded Nuovo Pasta Company 1989, which is a premier maker of fresh pasta in the nation.

By 1994 I had an itch to open a restaurant. I helped open an Asian-fusion restaurant in Greenwich called Baang with Jody Pennette, who taught me numerous valuable lessons; made a lot more contacts; and decided I loved the restaurant business. I especially appreciated meeting the architect Bruce Beinfield, who at the time was developing a building in South Norwalk. What a perfect locale for the tapas restaurant I had dreamed of since my days in Spain.

I contacted Andy Pforzheimer, who at the time was a colleague but not a business partner, showed him the space, and talked up the tapas concept. He loved it. We decided to take the plunge, and so, in 1996, the first Barcelona Restaurant and Wine Bar opened its doors. A highly trained chef, Andy oversaw the menu, and I took care of the design and overall ambience. Today our roles intermingle and are far from static, the two of us sharing equally in the excitement and energy that define all six Barcelona restaurants. Our dream of warm, welcoming places with great wine lists and small plates of tantalizing food that can be eaten as easily at the bar as at a table was realized. What could be better?

andy's story

I tell anyone who asks that the best way to break into the restaurant business is to beg for your first job. You may not earn anything, but you will learn something—perhaps even a lot—and you will have something for a résumé.

This is how I got started, and it has worked for me over and over. When I was in college, I had a job at the local Paco's Tacos in Cambridge, Massachusetts, and while that didn't exactly inspire me, I was interested enough in food to prepare weekly dinners for the *Harvard Lampoon*. After a wild eating tour of New Orleans during a summer vacation,

I decided to take a leave of absence from school and learn to cook in France. "Why not?" I thought. Isn't France where all the great chefs are?

I wrote to Chef André Parra, who owned L'Ermitage de Corton in Burgundy and who was a friend of a family friend, and then took off. After bicycling through the countryside for a few weeks, I ended up at the restaurant. I was summarily dismissed. André could not hire me; I had no work permit; he was well staffed; I knew nothing. I persuaded him to let me stay and teach his daughter English—and prep some food on the side.

I was nineteen and wanted to be there, which worked in my favor, as most of the apprentices were 16 and wanted to race motorcycles. I eventually worked my way up the ladder until I was the *chef poissonier* at L'Ermitage, a Michelin-starred restaurant with an international reputation. I worked sixteen hours a day, six days a week, an experience that formed the foundation for everything I learned after that.

A year and a half later I was back at Harvard, fluent in French, feeling pretty confident about my culinary skills, and certain that I wanted a life in the kitchen. After graduation I flew to California, where Jeremiah Tower was opening Stars. Again, I was rebuffed. The chef wouldn't see me; he was too busy. Finally I persuaded someone in the front of the house to hand-carry my résumé to whoever was running the kitchen that day. Jeremiah himself appeared a few minutes later and hired me on the spot. Perhaps he did so because he was understaffed and overwhelmed by the wild success of the restaurant, or perhaps it was because we shared the Harvard experience, but it was a lucky break for me.

My two years at Stars taught me about cooking as nothing else had. I worked the line, and it's on the line that you acquire hands-on skills. I worked next to great cooks who were taking part in the California cooking revolution of the 1980s. After my time there I moved to Los Angeles, where I worked with Patrick Healy at Colette for about six months before I met Peter Morton, who hired me to consult for the very young Hard Rock Cafe chain. Both experiences were valuable for different reasons. At Hard Rock, I discovered how much fun the restaurant business could be. As a menu consultant, I could waltz into the kitchen, cook any old thing, carry it out to a table of pretty girls, and ask them what they thought.

Eventually I became lonely for the East Coast and so made my way back to New York. Everyone I had met out West raved about a new restaurant called Arcadia, and so, true to form, I arrived at the Manhattan restaurant unannounced and asked the woman sitting up front to take my résumé to the executive chef. As luck would have it, that woman was Anne Rosenzweig, the chef/owner of Arcadia. Definitely not cool of me, but Anne seemed amused, and the man next to her, who turned out to be her partner, told me that "the last thing in the world we need is another Ivy League chef." Ouch. As fortune would have it, though, Anne was very much interested in hiring a right-hand assistant. When she was hired to revamp the menu at the 21 Club, I was asked to concentrate on two things: an old-fashioned breakfast that could double as a "power breakfast" (this was the late 1980s) and a great burger.

From my days at Stars and at Hard Rock, I knew how to make a damn good hamburger. For the 21 Club, I took a cue from James Beard and stuffed the burger with a generous pat of butter. Anne added herbs to the butter. When we put the burger on the menu, it was such a hit it ended up as a cover story for the *New York Times Sunday Magazine*.

introduction

From the "21" I spent the next few years knocking around the globe—Morocco, the Philippines, six months traveling around the world—and gradually taking on the head chef job in some well-known restaurants in New York. By the time I was nearly thirty years old, I was running one on the Upper West Side, married with a baby, and tiring of the long hours—so when Martha Stewart asked me to be the food editor of her new magazine, *Martha Stewart Living,* I grabbed the chance. My wife and I moved to Connecticut, and I started working from nine to five.

As much as I liked the magazine and Martha herself, I very quickly tired of the slow pace of an office job. I needed to get back to a kitchen and a restaurant with its daily drama and sense of excitement. I started a catering company in my house and dabbled as a restaurant consultant. One of my first clients was Sasa, who had the idea to open a tapas bar. I was intrigued by him, by the location, and by the concept, which was new to me—and I offered to be his partner in this one *small* venture!

We never wanted a high-end, white-tablecloth restaurant, and yet we wanted to serve great food. The tapas concept seemed to meet these criteria, and as we built on it, we eventually added main courses and desserts to the menu. This converted us from a very casual tapas bar to a full-service restaurant with an emphasis on tapas.

I was the first chef at Barcelona, which only made sense at the time. After a year, Sasa and I hired chefs and I took on more of the day-to-day management. When we open new restaurants, I inevitably find myself back in the kitchen, making sure everyone gets the message from day one: we care as much about quality as they do at Per Se, even if we bang it out.

the barcelona cookbook

With *The Barcelona Cookbook* in hand, you can re-create in your own kitchen what we do every night of the week. Here you will find recipes to create a meal that can be as casual or elaborate as your mood, and your family and your friends will thank you. We hope to introduce you to a style of eating and cooking that might not be familiar but that will invigorate you with its palate of bold, exciting, and satisfying flavors and textures.

We are nothing if not fanatical about tapas and other Spanish-inspired dishes. We love this style of cooking more than any other, which is saying a lot since both of us have worked in numerous restaurants, traveled extensively, and find much to admire in all of the world's cuisines.

The food in this book is good entertaining food, and we hope it will move you to throw a few bashes, big or small. Once you experience our cold and hot tapas, our main courses and desserts, you will understand how flawlessly these dishes translate to gatherings of family and friends. When you give a party with our food, you will want to serve Spanish wine and some kickass cocktails too. It's all here: tasty recipes for food and cocktails, information on choosing Spanish wines, menus for several different tapas parties, and a photo essay devoted to an outdoor party that you will wish you had attended.

So gather your friends. Put on some lively music. Celebrate wine, food, and life with us, Barcelona-style.

chapter 1

Cocktails and Wine

A great tapas place is centered around its bar. In Spain this means a place that serves sherry wine and plenty of beer, with the odd whiskey thrown in. We try very hard to educate our patrons on what authentic Spanish tapas and the tapas experience are, but we make no effort to insist that the clientele drink the way they do in Spain. Masochists we aren't.

We approached our bar by offering drinks that we liked ourselves. We had twenty-five wines by the glass at the outset—today we have more than forty—and we spent a tremendous amount of time trying wines that nobody was selling in the United States, such as godellos, albariños, and reds from Navarra and Jumilla.

With a lot of hard work, and by kissing a few frogs, we found great wines at bargain prices that we wanted to introduce to an unknowing public. We wanted customers to ask the bartenders and waiters, "I don't know any of these wines. What do you recommend?" Today the majority of our customers don't look for a familiar midpriced California cabernet but instead know their Ribera del Dueros from their Riojas in a way that was scarcely imaginable back in 1996.

We have learned a lot about Spanish wine since we opened and offer our insights and recommendations for your own parties and simple meals on pages 6 to 13. But beyond wine, our customers and your party guests like their drinks mixed. With Spain not providing much inspiration in the way of cocktails, we looked to South America: We took on mojitos and caipirinhas early, sometimes driving to New York to get cachaça when nobody in Connecticut carried it. Gradually we created a specialty drink list, a potent mix of the accumulated wisdom of transient bartenders and the enthusiastic reception of longtime customers. Those are what you will find in this chapter.

Try serving one or two cocktails at your next party. Everyone will love the excitement they provide. It's probably not a good idea to try to make more than two cocktails in one evening, as they are labor intensive and have to be made by the drink. On the other hand, a pitcher of ice-cold sangria is easy and always welcome to augment the cocktails at any party.

Caipirinha

Serves 1

½ lime, quartered

1 tablespoon sugar

2 ounces Lebron or other cachaça

2 tablespoons lemon-lime soda

1. In a small bowl, mix the lime and sugar and with the back of a spoon or a muddler, push on the lime pieces to crush them into the sugar, or to "muddle" them. Transfer to a cocktail shaker.

2. Fill the shaker with ice cubes, add the cachaça, and shake 5 to 7 times. Pour into a highball glass.

3. Pour the soda into the shaker and swirl to pick up the remaining lime and sugar. Top off the cocktail with the soda and serve.

Clementine Crush

Serves 1

¼ cup freshly squeezed orange juice

2 ounces Svedka Clementine vodka

2 tablespoons lemon-lime soda

1. Pour the juice and vodka into a shaker filled with ice. Shake 3 to 5 times. Pour into a highball glass.

2. Top off with the soda and serve.

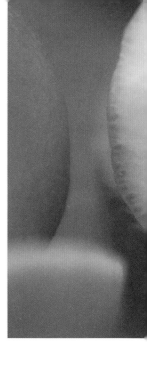

Red Sangria

Makes about 3 quarts, serving 6 to 8

Three 750 ml bottles red wine, such as Rioja or California zinfandel

½ cup brandy

⅓ cup light rum

⅓ cup Licor 43 or Triple Sec

⅓ cup amaretto

⅓ cup tequila

2 cups freshly squeezed orange juice

2 cups lemon-lime soda

About 2 cups sliced fresh fruit (such as oranges, green apples, grapefruit, pears, or strawberries) for garnish

1. In a very large pitcher or bowl (you might need 2 pitchers), mix together the red wine, brandy, rum, Licor 43, amaretto, and tequila. Add the orange juice and soda and stir to combine.

2. Pour into tall glasses filled with ice. Garnish with fresh fruit and serve.

White Sangria

Makes about 2 quarts, serving 4 to 6

Two 750 ml bottles crisp white
wine, such as albariño

⅓ cup peach schnapps

⅓ cup apricot brandy

2 cups lemon-lime soda

¼ cup peach puree, nectar, or juice

About 2 cups sliced fresh fruit (such as
oranges, tart green apples, peaches,
nectarines, or plums), for garnish

1. In a very large pitcher or bowl (you might need 2 pitchers), mix
together the white wine, schnapps, and brandy. Add the soda and
peach puree and stir to combine.

2. Pour into tall glasses filled with ice. Garnish with fresh fruit
and serve.

SPANISH WINE

As Spanish cuisine makes its way into America's mainstream, the Spanish wine world is emerging as one of the connoisseurs' favorite new frontiers. Wine drinkers across America have reason to celebrate, as wines and sherries from Spain are a treat to explore and to pour with our food.

Much of the wine that arrives on our shores from Spain seems new, fresh, and unknown, but ironically Spain has been producing wines since the days of the Roman Empire. It wasn't until about thirty years ago, however, that any of the vintages made more than a few ripples on the international scene. The exception are the famed sherry wines from southern Spain.

At Barcelona we know that many of our guests are seeking an exciting dining experience but may not know much about the food or wine of Spain. While it's relatively simple for them to decide what they might like from our tapas menu, the wine list often perplexes the average wine drinker. Therefore, to meet the demands of our ever-growing customer base, we instituted staff wine training in 2006. Every week Gretchen Thomas teaches classes on the wine regions of the world, different varietals and their characteristics, and the right choices for our menu offerings. She even gives quizzes. Hard ones! The best students in these classes become the restaurant's "wine steward," with the responsibility of keeping their knowledge current. So now, our waiters know even more about Spanish wines and how to pair them with our food.

Home cooks and party hosts may also want to pair Spanish wines with Spanish food for a full experience. Many of us think only of sangria when we consider Spanish wines, or perhaps we wonder about serving sherry. These are wonderful choices, but there is far, far more to Iberian wines. The next time you plan a party or casual get-together, try Spanish wines using the guidelines that follow. You won't be disappointed.

pairing wine with food

At Barcelona, our customers choose several different cold and hot tapas to combine and share as a meal with friends and family. It's tricky to choose one wine to pair with several different meats, vegetables, fish, and sauces, which is why we have a wine director. Gretchen oversees five wine stewards, one at each restaurant. She works with the stewards so that everyone is up on all the wines and menu items and can help our customers have the best eating and drinking experience possible.

Here Gretchen describes the four categories of Spanish wine, starting with sherry, going to white wine, cava (sparkling wine), and red wine. These characterizations will help ease the pain of decision making.

1. **SHERRY:** Sherry is the oft-overlooked fortified wine from southern Spain that actually is one of the ideal beverages to pair with Spanish food. In the United States, many of us are familiar only with the sweet cream sherries, if we know sherry at all. In Spain it is customary to drink the drier-style sherries with savory food. Here are several styles of dry sherry and their best pairings:

   - Fino is the lightest and driest of the sherry styles. It is pale, straw yellow, with distinct tangy, nutty aromas. Fino sherry pairs beautifully with olives, boquerones (anchovies), almonds, and Serrano ham. As a rule of thumb, fino can stand next to anything that is either briny or salty when other wines cannot.
   - Manzanilla is the same overall style and product as fino, but Manzanilla is made only in Sanlúcar de Barrameda. Fino is produced anywhere in the province of Jerez. Pair them with the same foods.
   - Amontillado sherries have more body, alcohol, and color than finos and Manzanilla. They have undergone some oxidation, which gives them their beautiful amber color and hazelnut aroma.

They can be reminiscent of a fine whiskey, without the high alcohol content. This style of sherry pairs well with fresh chorizo, Manchego cheese, and dried fruits, especially figs. We especially love amontillado with our sausage-stuffed piquillo peppers.

   - Oloroso is the least dry of these sherries and has a mahogany color, as well as a rich walnut aroma and silky texture. These sherries are fantastic with braised or grilled red meats and are dynamite with a fine cigar.

2. **WHITE WINE:** When your meal is laced with garlic, onions, vinegar, and spice, think white. Many of the tapas on our menu have strong flavors, such as Gambas al Ajillo, Grilled Steak Paillard, Mussels al Diablo, and Grilled Octopus Salad. Regardless of whether the main ingredient is fish or meat, the main flavor is what accompanies the protein and can often be harsh next to a heavy or oaky red wine. Clean and crisp white wines such as a godello or Txakolina will have the right amount of acidity to cut through any garlic or spice, plus the right body to enhance the food rather than overpower it.

3. **CAVA:** When in doubt, choose cava, the sparkling wine of Spain made in the traditional method. It is often referred to as the "poor man's Champagne," but we like to think of it as "the smart man's Champagne." Made from native varietals, cava can be just as acidic, fleshy, and yeasty as many top Champagnes, but typically always at a much lower cost. The reasonable cost is due to several factors, including a much steadier grape-growing climate (Champagne, France, is one of the coldest wine-producing regions in the world). Cava also has less of a reputation as a luxury good. Because of the carbonation, sparkling wines are the most overall food-friendly wines on the planet. Those tiny bubbles cut through the fattiest piece of steak as well as complement any delicate fish. So, when pairing with a large array of tapas or food styles, cava is a hands-down winner.

4. RED WINE: As for the red wines of Spain, follow this easy rule: If anything in the dish is smoked or the dish contains smoked paprika (such as Spanish chorizo), stick with the unoaked or lightly oaked red wines. Smoke in the food and smoke in the wine is, simply put, too much smoke. However, if planning on grilling or braising beef or lamb, the rich and oak barrel–aged red wines of Spain, especially of the tempranillo variety, are excellent companions for those rich red meats.

developing an appreciation for spanish wine

When we opened our doors in 1996, our customers were still enchanted with California wine, for both its style and its value. Back then these wines were most of what was available, and we worked hard to assemble a humble selection of forty wines from Spain. Now, with the rapidly rising cost of California wines, along with our customers' interest in new flavors and wine styles, our wine list has shrunk when it comes to the number of listings, but we now offer 120 Spanish wines spread over many appellations.

Our approach is simple: you tell us what you normally appreciate in a wine, and we will guide you to a vintage from Spain with the same profile. The majority of our customers are California-wine drinkers, and so they often associate the kinds of wines they prefer with specific varietals such as cabernet sauvignon, chardonnay, merlot, and pinot noir. Much to the surprise of many, more than these four varietals are planted in the world. In fact, there are thousands. Spain is an Old World wine region (as are all regions that belong to the European Union) and defines its wine types and styles based on the district where the grapes are grown and the wine is produced, as opposed to simply by the varietal. This bewilders the American consumer. It's not unusual for an avid lover of Napa Valley cabernet sauvignons to be disappointed with a cab from Penèdes, Spain. But that is why we are here to help.

for the cabernet sauvignon drinker

So what exactly are cabernet lovers looking for in a Spanish wine? They crave intensity, with three very important factors: oak, alcohol, and fruit, preferably all at high levels. Until about ten years ago, finding an equivalent from Spain was difficult, but now, with a new crop of young University of California–Davis trained winemakers rooting themselves in Europe, the internationalization of wine is becoming more and more of a reality. There are several emerging wine regions in Spain that are known for their intense red wines, the most important ones being Ribera del Duero, Toro, and Priorat.

Ribera del Duero is home of Vega Sicilia, a winery that pioneered the addition of cabernet sauvignon, merlot, and Malbec to the indigenous tempranillo variety (think Super Tuscan meets Spain). Vega Sicilia has become one of the most sought-after and expensive wines produced in Spain and has set the standard for what consumers worldwide expect from a Ribera red. While most wineries in the region stick to using 100 percent tempranillo-based wines, the wines are always intense, beautifully ripe, aged in either French or American oak barrels, and generally higher than 13 percent alcohol. We have a few wines that are favorites with our cabernet-drinking customers:

- Viña Solorca—The "Gran Solorca Reserva" is definitely one of the greatest values out of the entire region.
- Hacienda Monasterio—Famed winemaker Peter Sissek has taken on the project of blending the legal French varietals (cabernet sauvignon, malbec, merlot) in the tempranillo-based wine. The result is very comparable to Vega Sicilia, but without as high a price.
- Bodegas Aalto—Mariano Garcia was the winemaker of Vega Sicilia for nearly thirty years before leaving to start his own project. Aalto is an incredibly ripe and layered tempranillo wine that never disappoints the Napa Valley aficionados.

The tiny region of Toro, which lies west of Ribera along the Duero River valley, produces mostly red wines that are generally 100 percent tempranillo. Toro reds carry distinct, consistent mocha aromas and flavors, as compared to the many other tempranillo wines of northern Spain. Although a lesser-known region, Toro has a few of its own accolade-garnering wineries, most notably San Roman and Bodegas Numanthia-Termes. While the wines fetch some incredibly high prices, most of the powerful tempranillo wines represent some of Spain's top-value reds. A few of the ones we recommend are:

- Juan Rojo—A rich and full-bodied tempranillo made by one of Spain's many emerging female winemakers, Rosa Zarza.
- Prima—Another project of Mariano Garcia, this wine delivers powerful ripeness and tannins at a strikingly low price point.

The third region that would satisfy the palates of the cabernet sauvignon drinker is the tiny region of Priorat. Located in Catalunya, just inland and over the mountains from Barcelona, Priorat has earned cultlike status in the wine world owing to its unique terraced vineyards and black slate soil. The "terroir" of this region renders the area nearly useless for cultivating anything other than grapevines; many describe the landscape as resembling a moonscape.

A handful of French and Spanish winemakers decided to revive the area's once dead wine-producing culture in the late 1980s and bought up all the native old-vine garnacha (known as grenache in the south of France and the rest of the world) and Cariñena. They planted vineyards with cabernet sauvignon, merlot, and syrah grapes. Most of the wineries produce only a few hundred cases of wine a year; the soil makes the vines difficult to cultivate, so they produce low yields. But the wines are unsurpassed in strength and age-ability. Typically, the sweet and licorice garnacha is blended with earthy and dry cabernet sauvignon, delivering powerful tannins and body. In fact, the wine can't even be labeled Priorat

unless it reaches at least 14.5 percent alcohol. While never inexpensive, Priorat reds are unforgettably complex and make our customers just as fanatic as we are.

- "Marge," Celler de l'Encastell—This wine has become a staff favorite in our Norwalk location. One of the less expensive examples from this region, the Marge packs beautiful ripe and spicy aromas in a full-bodied package.
- "Solanes," Cims de Porrera—One of the only producers that bases the wine with more Cariñena than garnacha, the wine has a dusty dryness, which appeals to our Rutherford-loving wine guests.
- Clos Erasmus—This wine is made by one of the most prestigious winemakers in the region, Daphne Glorian. It was one of the first wines to catch the attention of wine critics worldwide. Barcelona Wine Bar receives only a tiny allocation of the 140 cases produced each year.

for the pinot noir drinker

While cabernet sauvignon drinkers often dominate our wine-drinking customers, there is another popular red varietal that represents the other end of the flavor and style spectrum: pinot noir. Originally famous for the light, complex, and earth-driven wines from Burgundy, France, pinot noir grapes are now planted all over the world (not always successfully) and deliver a spectrum of wine styles. While California's Santa Barbara Valley produces the most ripe, intense, and spicy pinots on the West Coast, Oregon's Willamette Valley creates a light and elegantly styled wine. Spain is not exactly a pinot noir–producing country, and so Rioja is the best-known red wine–producing area that makes lighter-bodied yet complex wines.

Rioja is located in northern Spain, with its northernmost area considered a part of the Basque Country. Tempranillo is also the king varietal in this region, but it yields very different results compared to neighboring regions. Garnacha, mazuela, and graciano are all classic, native varietals, and all contribute to the final outcomes, depending on how successful the vintage was for tem-

pranillo. The real factor that gives Riojas their distinct flavor profile and lightness is the oak barrel and bottle aging. Traditionally, American oak has always been used for both fermentation and aging vessels, but many producers have switched to using French oak for a more modern approach. Riojas are classified by how long they age before market release and are titled accordingly:

- Crianza—This wine spends a minimum of one year in the barrel and one year in the bottle before release.
- Reserva—This wine spends a minimum of one year in the barrel and two years in the bottle before release.
- Gran Reserva—This wine spends a minimum of two years in the barrel and three years in the bottle before release.

What's the point? For a consumer, the idea is that no wine will be sold until it's ready to drink, as opposed to selling newly released classified Bordeaux that have to be stored for ten years at your own risk.

As the internationalization of wine spreads worldwide, regions like Rioja have become divided by those producers who continue to make wine in the classic style and those who take a more modern approach. The main difference is intensity. The classic wines, which still dominate the area's production, are lighter-bodied, bright, earthy, and low in tannin. The modern wines are substantially more concentrated and oaky, not too far from the style of Ribera del Duero reds. While our list has a few examples of the modern Rioja style, the majority are very Old World and are excellent substitutes for pinot noir. The best examples are:

- La Rioja Alta—While this is probably one of the most classic wineries in Rioja, it consistently holds back wines from release for many years longer than the required minimums. For instance, the current crianza vintage is 2000.
- El Coto de Imaz—This is one of the most recognizable Riojas in the United States. Coto de Imaz remains one of the best quality-for-value Riojas made in the classic style.

- C.V.N.E.— This is considered one of the giants of the Rioja producers. C.V.N.E. (pronounced coo-nay) has a few examples in both the classic and modern styles, all very impressive and age worthy.

for pinot grigio and sauvignon blanc drinkers

Our white-wine drinkers are often more difficult to please than the red-wine lovers due to the vast style difference between California and Spanish white wines. Spain, like all Old World wine region countries, manipulates the varietal expression of its white wines very little. This means brand-new oak barrels are rarely used and malolactic fermentation (an awful vocabulary word that means the process that gives wines their distinct buttery and creamy nature) is generally halted to protect the fresh acidity. This presents a few challenges for our servers and bartenders, because those who like California chardonnay don't always like the Spanish selections. However, for the pinot grigio and sauvignon blanc lovers, Spanish whites can be fantastically satisfying.

While red wine production definitely dominates the scene in Spain, one region creates some of the most beautiful white wines on the market and is very up-and-coming internationally. Galicia, located in the northwestern corner of Spain, produces the vast majority of white wines coming from the country, not only because its climate is the most suitable for white grapes but also because the local cuisine is dominated by fish and seafood. Galicia, which hugs the coast of the Atlantic, is also known as "green Spain" because its landscape and culture are much more akin to those of Ireland than to the rest of Spain—a far cry from what we Americans imagine as being typical.

While several indigenous grape varieties are grown in the wine regions of Galicia, albariño and godello are the two standouts. Albariño, thought to have some genetic ties to Riesling, produces a highly aromatic white wine that has boomed in popularity in recent years. It produces very floral and tropical fruit aromas, and the ones from the best vineyards have distinct minerality and age-ability. Rías Baixas, a tiny region just north of the

Portuguese border, is where most of Galicia's albariños are produced. Oak barrels are rarely used for fermenting or aging these wines, as it is believed that oak will clash with the natural beauty of the varietal, and so the wines are aged in stainless-steel barrels. A few producers experiment with used oak barrels to add subtle toast and vanilla notes to the wine. Some recommendations are:

- Pazo de Señoráns—This is definitely one of the top producers because of its old-vine albariño vineyards. The outstanding quality of the wine is worth the extra money.
- Lagar de Cervera—Owned by the La Rioja Alta family, this winery consistently impresses year after year.
- "Nora de Neve," Viña Nora—This is one of the few oak barrel–fermented albariños. It successfully balances floral and apple notes with a touch of toasty oak and is great for our California chardonnay lovers.

Godello presents quite a different profile from albariño. It, too, is grown all over Galicia, but it seems to have found its rightful home in Valdeorras, a region nestled between two mountain ranges in eastern Galicia. Godello never has the same aromatic potency as albariño, but at its best it can have the structure of Grand Cru Chablis. It is, for the time being, much more affordable. Because of its strong acid content, godello always seems the drier option of the two varietals. Our two favorites are:

- "Montenovo," Val de Sil—This is an inexpensive and refreshing white wine. It is fermented in stainless steel and is completely clean and crisp.
- "As Sortes," Rafael Palacios—This has become something of a cult wine and is another rare example of a white that is fermented in oak barrels. It is more like a Meursault from Burgundy, and the smoky aromas always please our California wine drinkers.

Overall, Spain offers a broad range of wine styles. We truly believe there is a Spanish wine in the market, and on our wine list, for every type of wine drinker out there. From the light-bodied, quaffable table wines and extremely extracted red wines to age-worthy premier cru Bordeaux–like wines, they are all coming out of Iberia. And there are many more to be discovered. Between the wines by the glass and the ever-expanding wine list, we love to get the buzz going about the latest great wines from Spain.

Effen Awesome

Serves 1

¼ cup pineapple juice

2 ounces black cherry vodka

1 ounce crème de cassis

1 maraschino cherry, for garnish

1. Pour the pineapple juice, vodka, and crème de cassis into a shaker filled with ice cubes. Shake 5 to 7 times and strain into a highball glass.

2. Garnish the cocktail with a cherry and serve.

Comforter

Serves 1

½ cup unsweetened cranberry juice

2 ounces Stoli Razberi vodka

1 tablespoon liquid sour mix

Pour all the ingredients into a shaker filled with ice cubes. Shake 5 to 7 times, pour into a highball glass, and serve.

Mr. Pats' Old-Fashioned Lemonade

Serves 1

½ lemon, quartered

1 tablespoon sugar

2 ounces Ketel One Citroen vodka

1 ounce curaçao

2 tablespoons lemon-lime soda

1. In a small bowl, mix the lemon and sugar. Using the back of a spoon or a muddler, push on the lemon pieces to crush them into the sugar, or "muddle" them. Transfer to a cocktail shaker.

2. Fill the shaker with ice cubes and add the vodka and curaçao. Shake 10 to 12 times and strain into a highball glass.

3. Pour the soda into the shaker and swirl to pick up the remaining lemon and sugar. Top off the cocktail with soda and serve.

the barcelona cookbook

Blood Orange Margarita

Serves 1

6 tablespoons freshly squeezed blood orange juice

1 ounce Cointreau

2 tablespoons freshly squeezed lime juice

½ ounce Patrón Silver tequila

1 tablespoon liquid sour mix

Margarita salt or other coarse salt, for salting the glass

Lime wedge

1. Pour the orange juice, Cointreau, lime juice, tequila, and sour mix into a shaker filled with ice cubes and shake 5 to 7 times.

2. Spread the salt on a plate. Rub the rim of a chilled highball glass with the lime wedge. Dip the rim of the glass in the salt to coat it.

3. Pour the margarita into the glass and serve.

Zaya Tai

Serves 1

2 ounces Zaya rum

¼ cup pineapple juice

1 ounce crème de banana liqueur

Pour all the ingredients into a shaker filled with ice cubes. Shake 5 to 7 times, pour into a highball glass, and serve.

Gazpacho Boracho

Serves 1

Freshly ground black pepper

6 tablespoons Barcelona Gazpacho (page 42) or other tomato-based gazpacho

2 ounces Tito's Handmade Vodka or other high-quality vodka

Dash of Tabasco sauce

1 rib celery or 1 slice cucumber, for garnish

1. Fill an 8-ounce highball glass with ice and sprinkle with pepper.

2. Pour the gazpacho and vodka into a shaker filled with ice. Add the Tabasco and shake 10 or 12 times. Strain into the glass, garnish with celery or cucumber, and serve.

Matador

Serves 1

3 ounces 1800 Silver tequila or other tequila

1 ounce blue curaçao

¼ cup unsweetened cranberry juice

1 tablespoon grenadine

Lemon-lime soda

1 lime wedge, for garnish

1. Pour the tequila, curaçao, cranberry juice, and grenadine into a shaker filled with ice cubes. Shake for 30 seconds and strain into a chilled martini glass.

2. Add a splash of soda, garnish the martini with the lime wedge, and serve.

Agave Martini

Serves 1

3 ounces Don Julio silver tequila or other tequila

2 tablespoons curaçao

¼ cup unsweetened cranberry juice

½ ounce Cointreau

Freshly squeezed lime juice

1 orange wedge, for garnish

1. Pour the tequila, curaçao, cranberry juice, and Cointreau into a shaker filled with ice cubes. Shake 10 to 12 times and strain into a chilled martini glass.

2. Add a splash of lime juice, garnish the martini with the orange slice, and serve.

Metrotini

Serves 1

2 ounces Svedka Clementine vodka

1 ounce Triple Sec

2 tablespoons freshly squeezed
blood orange juice

1 tablespoon freshly squeezed lime juice

1 thin slice blood orange, for garnish

1. Pour the vodka, Triple Sec, orange juice, and lime juice into a shaker filled with ice cubes. Shake 5 to 7 times and strain into a chilled martini glass.

2. Garnish with the blood orange slice and serve.

White Peach Martini

Serves 1

2 ounces Svedka Clementine vodka

1 ounce peach brandy

1 ounce DeKuyper Peachtree schnapps

2 tablespoons white peach puree (see Note)

1 thin slice fresh white peach

1. Pour the vodka, brandy, schnapps, and puree into a shaker filled with ice cubes. Shake 10 to 12 times and strain into a chilled martini glass.

2. Garnish the cocktail with a slice of white peach and serve.

Note: Peach puree is available at some liquor stores and specialty markets. If you can't find it or would prefer to make your own, mash a very ripe, peeled white peach with a fork to make a puree.

Mojito

Serves 1

½ lime, quartered

5 fresh mint leaves

1 tablespoon sugar

2 ounces Bacardi Limón rum

2 tablespoons club soda

1. In a small bowl, mix the lime, mint leaves, and sugar. Using the back of a spoon or a muddler, push on the lime pieces and mint leaves to crush them into the sugar, or "muddle" them. Transfer to a cocktail shaker.

2. Fill the shaker with ice cubes and add the rum. Shake 5 to 8 times and then pour into a highball glass.

3. Pour the club soda into the shaker and swirl to pick up the remaining lime, mint, and sugar. Top off the cocktail with soda and serve.

Martini Manzana Roja

Serves 1

2 ounces Zyr vodka

2 ounces Golden Ger Green Apple Liqueur

2 tablespoons liquid sour mix

2 tablespoons unsweetened cranberry juice

1 thin slice red-skinned apple, for garnish

1. Pour the vodka, apple liqueur, sour mix, and cranberry juice into a shaker filled with ice cubes. Shake 8 to 10 times and strain into a chilled martini glass.

2. Garnish with the apple slice and serve.

Pomegranate Martini

Serves 1

2 ounces Grey Goose vodka

1 ounce Triple Sec

2 tablespoons pomegranate juice

1 tablespoon freshly squeezed lime juice

5 pomegranate seeds, for garnish

1. Pour the vodka, Triple Sec, pomegranate juice, and lime juice into a shaker filled with ice cubes. Shake 10 to 12 times and strain into a chilled martini glass.

2. Garnish the cocktail with the pomegranate seeds and serve.

TAPAS

SAL
SERRANO:M
Manchego:R
Narcona:M
Boquerones:

chapter 2

Cold Tapas

In Spain, most tapas are served at room temperature, usually from behind or on top of a bar. Some are served on pieces of bread; some are on toothpicks; some are what we call "scoop and serve." They are no more a sit-down meal than a pretzel would be on the streets of New York. They are meant to leaven the sherry and beer drinking that occupies the midafternoon or the all-important time between the end of work and the beginning of dinner.

With the creation of the Barcelona Restaurants and Wine Bars, we set out to educate the American eater in how to enjoy tapas: sit at the bar, enjoy some small plates, and have a glass of wine. This style of eating was new to the American eater, and we often heard, "Where are the waiters? Where is the menu? Where are the tables?" In response, we turned the hamburger joint next door (which we also owned

at the time) into a dining room and started offering table service, along with a rudimentary menu. At the beginning, cold tapas were the majority of what we served. With a kitchen at our disposal, we began to invent hot tapas, which looked more like tiny appetizers.

Still, when we opened in 1996, not too many of our customers got it. They were curious about the tapas, were

game to try them, and eventually they came to appreciate them as much as we do. Most of our customers now come to Barcelona for the tapas. Clearly these dishes are our signature, and the wide choice of good Spanish wines we offer only enhances the experience.

Nowadays, tapas are almost commonplace in America. Many people have traveled to Spain, where they have tried them, and many more have read about them in food magazines, in cookbooks, and on the Internet, or have heard about them on the Food Network. Tapas bars have sprung up in every city from New York to San Francisco, some far better than others.

Our cold tapas are really three distinct types of dishes. Some are salads, either simple or composed. Some are made for fast service and casual presentation, what we call "scoop and serve." And the third type are artfully prepared cold dishes, fancy-restaurant choices in miniature. All of these

styles are ideal for large-scale entertaining. No matter how adventurous you feel about making dinner, nothing relieves the pressure like a table of dishes ready to serve during the cocktail hour, to arrange on an elaborate buffet, or to pass around the table before the main course.

Cold tapas, more than any other part of this book, are ingredient driven. You can change the flavor of a shrimp by sautéing it with garlic, but a *boquerón* or a piquillo pepper is naked on a cold dish. Be sure to select quality ingredients, because the drizzle of olive oil on top won't disguise lesser quality. There are now quite a few good Internet and mail-order sources for top-notch Spanish ingredients (see page 197). Thanks to the Spanish love of all things preserved and canned, you can use these sources for almost everything in this book. When it comes to salads, though, buy fresh, use soon, and be generous with the olive oil.

Roasted Olives

You wouldn't think it would be too hard to come up with a mix of olives to serve. In fact, it took us three years to come up with the right blend, and we are still vigilant. When the plates go out, cooks like to grab the biggest olives first, which means the last plates of the night tend to be filled with small Niçoise and Arbequina olives. Although we have to make sure our customers receive the variety we intended, you won't have this problem when you serve your guests, who will love these dressed-up olives.

Serves 4 to 6

1 red bell pepper

1 tablespoon olive oil

4 cups assorted olives with pits (such as kalamata, Niçoise, Arbequina, Cerignola, picholine, and oil-cured black olives), drained and patted dry

7 sprigs fresh thyme, quartered

4 sprigs fresh rosemary, quartered

6 whole cloves garlic, peeled

Julienned zest of 1 orange

¼ teaspoon hot red pepper flakes

¼ cup red wine vinegar

¼ cup sherry vinegar

¾ cup extra-virgin olive oil

1. Preheat the oven to 450°F.

2. Rub the bell pepper with the tablespoon of olive oil. Lay the pepper on a baking sheet and roast for 12 to 15 minutes, or until the side of the pepper resting on the baking sheet is wrinkled and almost black. Turn the pepper over and continue roasting for 7 to 8 minutes longer, or until the pepper is nicely charred on all sides.

3. Transfer the pepper to a small bowl and cover the bowl with plastic wrap. Let the pepper steam as it cools in the bowl for about 10 minutes. Remove from the bowl, rub off the charred skin, open the pepper, and scrape out the seeds and membranes. Cut the pepper into very thin strips (about ⅛ inch thick).

4. Reduce the oven temperature to 425°F.

5. In a large mixing bowl, mix together the olives, julienned red pepper, thyme, rosemary, garlic, orange zest, and pepper flakes. Toss well. Add the red wine vinegar and sherry vinegar to the olives and stir to distribute evenly.

6. Spread the olives on a jelly roll or shallow roasting pan. Roast for about 35 minutes, stirring frequently, or until the olives are tender. To test for doneness, taste an olive to see if the meat separates easily from the pit. If so, the olives are done.

7. Let the olives cool in the pan. When cool, drizzle with the extra-virgin olive oil and stir to mix. Serve right away or refrigerate in a container with a tight-fitting lid for up to 5 days.

8. Remove the olives from the refrigerator at least 2 hours before serving to let them reach room temperature. Stir well before serving.

Roasted Beets with Cabrales and Toasted Walnuts

This is one of the first tapas we ever made, back in the original Norwalk barroom in 1996. Then it was almost impossible to find good Spanish blue cheese, and we went back and forth from Cabrales to Valdeón, depending on what was available and tasted best. These days we prefer Valdeón, but both are acceptable. If your market doesn't carry Spanish blues, any good blue cheese will work well.

The secret to the beets' flavor is to toss them with good Japanese rice wine vinegar while they are still hot. No other kind of vinegar works when it comes to complementing and capturing the sweetness of the beets. Andy stole this trick from well-known San Francisco chef Jeremiah Tower. If you refrigerate the beets, let them return to room temperature before you serve them.

Serves 4

3 pounds red beets, tops removed

⅓ cup rice wine vinegar

¼ pound Cabrales or other blue cheese (such as Roquefort)

½ cup chopped toasted walnuts (see Note)

Chopped fresh flat-leaf parsley, for garnish

Sea salt, for garnish

1. Preheat the oven to 450°F.

2. Cut six 5 by 7-inch pieces of aluminum foil. Put 2 to 3 beets in the center of each sheet, making sure there is plenty of extra foil to work with.

3. Bring the sides of the foil sheets together and fold to form a package. Put the packages directly on the center rack of the oven and roast for about 1½ hours, or until a knife can easily be inserted in the largest beet. Let the beets sit in the packages until they are cool enough to handle.

4. Using a clean kitchen towel (choose one you don't mind getting stained), rub each beet to remove the skin. Cut the peeled beets into rough dice measuring about 1½ inches square.

5. Transfer the beets to a mixing bowl and toss with the rice vinegar. Transfer to a container with a tight-fitting lid and refrigerate for up to 2 days before continuing.

6. Divide the beets among 4 serving plates or arrange them on a serving platter. Crumble the blue cheese over the beets and then top with the walnuts and parsley. Garnish with sea salt and serve.

Note: To toast the walnuts, spread about ½ cup shelled walnuts in a single layer on a baking sheet. Roast in a 400°F oven for about 10 minutes, stirring once or twice, until lightly browned. When the nuts are cool, chop them coarsely.

OUR SIGNATURE DISH

Tapas have been a Spanish tradition for generations. Eating them is a ritual in Spain, and in fact the term de tapeo means "barhopping." In Spain, bars are called tascas, and each one serves its own special tapas. They are meant to be eaten while you stand at the bar and are only one or two bites. Groups of friendly Spaniards will meet at a tasca for lunch or at the end of the day and order a small beer (a zurito) or glass of wine and an assortment of that bar's tapas. In the evening, after an hour or so, they move on to the next bar for another round of tapas and drinks. And so it goes, often into the small hours, or until it's late enough for a proper Spanish dinner.

Tapas are rarely prepared at home in Spain, although we don't subscribe to the ban. Americans love to give tapas parties, and we like to cater them when asked. With the recipes here, you can give a party with an assortment of cold and hot tapas, pitchers of icy sangria, and perhaps a simple cake or flan for dessert. And don't forget the flamenco music.

By any other name, a tapa is an antipasto, hors d'oeuvre, or meze. Just about every culture has a number of dishes that precede the main course, often meant to be enjoyed with alcohol and always to whet the appetite.

Tapas can be as simple as a slice of chorizo and a piece of cheese, a few roasted olives, one or two grilled sardines or pencil-slim spring asparagus. They can be as elaborate as a hot cazuela of sizzling shrimp in garlic and oil or an empanada filled with spiced meat and served with roasted pepper sauce. When the food is served on a piece of bread, the tapa is called a montadito, and when a small roll is split and filled, the tapa is called a pulguita. In the Basque country, tapas are called pintxos (also spelled pinchos). The term derives from the Spanish word *pinchar*, or "to prick," because typically Basque tapas were served on small skewers and many still are. (The bars in San Sebastian and Bilbao still charge by the toothpick.)

The origin of tapas is not known, although they most likely were first served in southern Spain. The word tapar means "to cover," and so the term tapas might derive from a custom of serving a small bite with a glass of wine or beer, perhaps balanced on top of the glass to avoid using a plate. The other explanation is that they were set out at the bar and covered to keep the flies off. Tapas were meant to be eaten with the fingers, but many that we—and other restaurants here and in Spain—serve require a knife and fork, which does not make them any less tasty.

Filet Mignon with Horseradish Cream on Toasted Ficelle

The black pepper rub on the filets is what gives them flavor, and the salt in the rub ensures that the peppercorns, rosemary, and garlic get below the surface of the meat. This cold sliced filet was one of our original tapas, which we used to serve with sautéed wild mushrooms. The mushrooms eventually ended up in the mushroom and herbed cheese dish on page 90. The filet mignon became a main course on our menu, where it has remained for the last decade. It's a terrific hors d'oeuvre or tapa and a little more filling than others.

Serves 4

Filet Mignon

2 tablespoons black peppercorns

3 teaspoons dried rosemary

2 tablespoons kosher salt

2 cloves garlic, coarsely chopped

¼ cup olive oil

One 12-ounce piece filet mignon (beef tenderloin)

Horseradish Cream

½ cup sour cream

3 tablespoons bottled horseradish

Pinch of kosher salt

Ficelle

1 long, narrow baguette (about 2 inches in diameter)

¼ cup olive oil

Sea salt, for garnish

1. For the filet mignon: In a spice grinder or a mortar and pestle, grind or crush the peppercorns and rosemary to a fine powder. Add the salt and stir to mix. Add the garlic and blend to a paste.

2. In a small bowl, stir the spice mixture into ¼ cup olive oil. Rub the paste on both sides of the tenderloin. Wrap the meat in plastic wrap and refrigerate for at least 6 hours and up to 2 days.

3. For the horseradish cream: In a small mixing bowl, stir together the sour cream and horseradish. Season with salt and stir well. Cover and refrigerate until needed or for up to 3 days.

4. Preheat the oven to 425°F.

5. For the ficelle: Slice the bread into 25 to 30 slices about ¼ inch thick. Brush with the other ¼ cup olive oil to coat both sides. Lay the slices on a baking sheet. Toast the bread in the oven for about 7 minutes. Rotate the baking sheet and toast for 3 minutes longer, or until the bread slices are crisp and browned. Let the ficelle cool.

6. Remove the tenderloin from the refrigerator and scrape the spice cure from it. Season with a little salt.

7. Heat an ovenproof sauté pan over high heat and sear the tenderloin on all sides until lightly browned. Transfer the pan to the oven and cook for about 7 minutes longer for medium-rare, or to the desired degree of doneness. Remove the tenderloin from the pan and set aside to rest and cool for about 20 minutes.

8. Slice the tenderloin into slices about ¼ inch thick.

9. Spread each ficelle with about 1 teaspoon of horseradish cream and top each with a slice of meat. Garnish each with a pinch of sea salt and serve.

Tuna Tartare with Yuca Chips

Sasa likes to say that "typical" Barcelona restaurants like to serve sushi and smoked salmon, just like their counterparts in Milan, London, or New York. When he suggested tuna tartare, Andy thought it might be too expensive and too "French" for the Barcelona menu. We ran it as a special, sold out, and have been unable to take it off the menu for the past ten years.

We prepare tuna tartare in several different ways, including an Asian version. The key is to start with *really* good, fresh tuna, enough good olive oil, and just enough lemon, salt, and mustard to give it character, but never to overpower it.

Serves 4

¾ pound sushi-grade
tuna loin, chilled

1½ tablespoons chopped fresh
chives, plus chives for garnish

2 teaspoons extra-virgin olive oil

1½ teaspoons drained capers

1½ teaspoons Dijon mustard

¼ teaspoon freshly
squeezed lemon juice

3 pinches of kosher salt,
or more to taste

32 to 36 Yuca Chips (recipe follows)

1. Separate the tip of the loin from the bottom by cutting through it horizontally, with the top portion being two-thirds of the whole, and the bottom being one-third. Separate the two parts. The bottom piece has the sinew and skin. Put the thinner, bottom piece of tuna in the refrigerator to keep it cold as you work with the thicker, top piece.

2. Using a very sharp knife, slice the loin into strips about ⅛ inch thick. Cut these crosswise into dice about ⅛ inch wide. Transfer the tuna to a medium bowl, cover, and refrigerate to chill the tuna. It's important to keep the tuna as cold as possible.

3. Take the bottom piece of tuna from the refrigerator, and using a large spoon, scrape the tuna downward to free the meat from the sinew. Chop the scraped meat and add it to the refrigerated diced tuna. Discard the sinews and skin.

4. Add the chives, olive oil, capers, mustard, lemon juice, and salt to the tuna. Stir gently to mix. Taste and add more salt if necessary.

5. Set a 4-inch ring mold on 1 of 4 serving plates and pack about a quarter of the tartare in the mold. Lift the mold off the tartare and then garnish the plate with 8 or 9 yuca chips and some chopped chives. Repeat with the other 3 servings and serve immediately.

yuca chips   We serve these with the tuna tartare as they are very subtle and don't fight with the tartare's flavor. They are satisfying to make, and we're sure you will find many other ways to serve them, with other seafood, soup, salads, and dips.

Yuca is a large root that usually is 8 to 10 inches long and 2 to 3 inches in diameter, with a brown outer skin and crisp, white flesh. It should be firm and smooth and smell clean and fresh. When yuca is off, it has a distinctive, unpleasant odor. Look for it alongside other root vegetables such as jícama, turnips, and potatoes. Once peeled, store it in the refrigerator and be sure to core it before using.

Makes about 36 chips

1 yuca

5 cups canola oil

Kosher salt

1. Peel the yuca and slice in half crosswise. Using a mandoline, slice the yuca about 1/16 inch thick and immediately plunge the slices into a bowl of ice water while slicing the rest. If you don't have a mandoline, use a small sharp knife and slice the yuca as thin as possible.

2. When all the yuca is sliced, drain and pat the slices dry with a clean kitchen cloth.

3. Meanwhile, in a deep, heavy pot, slowly heat the canola oil to 400°F. Line a baking sheet with paper towels and put it close to the pot.

4. Working in batches, fry only a few of the yuca slices for 4 to 5 minutes or until crisp. The yuca will not brown as they fry and should be removed from the oil as soon as they are crisp.

5. Lift the yuca chips from the oil with a slotted spoon and transfer to the paper towel–lined pan to drain. While warm, season lightly with salt.

6. When cool, store the chips in an airtight container for up to 2 days.

Citrus Seviche

Seviche is not Spanish, but we had a chef a number of years ago named John Strong who came to us from a Cuban-fusion restaurant and made wonderful seviche. It fulfills a lot of requirements for a restaurant such as ours: it is exotic, easy to pick up, and uses extra shrimp when *gambas'* sales are slow. The orange rounds out the citrus and keeps the dish from "overcooking," which is what lemon and lime will do over time. The better the quality of the seafood you use, the better the seviche will taste.

Serves 6

Shrimp and Scallops

1 carrot, peeled and coarsely chopped

1 rib celery, coarsely chopped

½ Spanish onion, coarsely chopped

2 teaspoons sherry vinegar

2 bay leaves

1 teaspoon kosher salt

½ pound pink or white shrimp (21–25 count)

½ pound giant dry scallops

Marinade

Juice of 4 oranges

Juice of 2 lemons

Juice of 1 lime

4 whole oranges

1 whole lemon

1 whole lime

1 red bell pepper, seeded, cored, and sliced into ¼-inch-wide strips

1 green bell pepper, seeded, cored, and sliced into ¼-inch-wide strips

1 plum tomato, thinly sliced

1 red onion, very thinly sliced (preferably with a mandoline)

1 jalapeño pepper, very thinly sliced

½ bunch cilantro, thick stems removed, leaves and small stems finely chopped

Kosher salt

Extra-virgin olive oil, for drizzling

1. For the shrimp and scallops: Put the carrot, celery and onion in a medium saucepan and add enough water to cover by an inch or two. Add the sherry, bay leaves, and salt and bring to a simmer over medium-high heat. Cook for about 40 minutes, adjusting the heat up or down to maintain the simmer.

2. Peel the shrimp and remove the tails. Slit each along the inside curve and rinse under cool running water.

3. Remove and discard the muscle from the scallops and cut each scallop in half horizontally.

4. Drop the shrimp into the simmering broth and blanch for about 4 minutes, or until opaque. With a slotted spoon, lift the shrimp from the broth and lay on a baking sheet in a single layer to cool.

5. Drop the scallops into the simmering broth and blanch for about 3 minutes, or until opaque. Lift the scallops from the broth and lay on the baking sheet with the shrimp. Transfer the baking sheet to the refrigerator for at least 3 hours, until cold, or for up to 24 hours. There is no need to cover the seafood.

6. For the marinade: In a small bowl, stir together the orange, lemon, and lime juices.

7. Remove the skin from the whole oranges, the lemon, and the lime and, holding the fruit over the bowl to catch the juices, cut between the segments. Remove any white pith and then drop the segments into the juice.

8. Add the bell peppers, tomato, onion, jalapeño, and cilantro to the bowl and season to taste with salt.

9. Add the chilled seafood to the marinade. Toss well, cover, and refrigerate for at least 2 hours or up to 12 hours to allow the seafood to "cook" in the marinade.

10. Adjust the seasoning with salt. Serve in chilled bowls and drizzle with extra-virgin olive oil.

Ensalada Mixta

When Andy learned to make salads in California and France, he always tossed them with the dressing in a bowl and then served them. Sasa preferred serving them the way he ate them in Argentina: big chunks of lettuce, tomato, and onion with oil and vinegar drizzled on them at the last minute. We argued about this for a while, and Sasa won. Later, when we traveled to Argentina together, Sasa enjoyed taunting Andy over and over with, "Doesn't this salad taste good?" Andy had to agree; it did.

Serves 4 to 6

3 heads romaine lettuce

½ Spanish onion, thinly sliced into rings

1 pint ripe plum cherry tomatoes, quartered

¾ cup assorted green and black olives

6 tablespoons extra-virgin olive oil

2 tablespoons aged sherry vinegar

Sea salt and freshly cracked black pepper

1. Trim about ½ inch from the top of the heads of lettuce and then cut the lettuce leaves into ¾-inch-long pieces. Transfer to a serving platter and top with the onion slices. Arrange the tomato quarters and olives randomly on the lettuce.

2. Drizzle the olive oil and then the vinegar over the lettuce and tomatoes. Season to taste with salt and pepper and serve.

Mashed Sardines

This is tapa-as-snack. In Spain, many tapas are very quick, small bites. Ours are more like little appetizers, meant to be shared. We serve this mashed sardine dish plated, but really it is best served on little croutons before dinner.

Serves 6

Two 8-ounce cans good-quality Spanish
sardines packed in olive oil, drained

¼ bunch fresh flat-leaf parsley, stems removed and leaves slivered

½ medium red onion, finely diced

Zest of ¼ lemon, finely chopped

Juice of ½ lemon

1 teaspoon extra-virgin olive oil

Slices of toasted baguette or crackers, for serving

1. In a medium mixing bowl, mash the sardines with a fork until they are the consistency of canned tuna. Add the parsley, onion, lemon zest, lemon juice, and olive oil and stir to mix well. Use immediately or cover and refrigerate for up to 2 days.

2. Serve the sardines on baguettes or crackers.

Barcelona Gazpacho

In Spain, there is no more agreement about what constitutes "correct" gazpacho than there is agreement about barbecue in the United States. This classic gazpacho has great flavor and is preferred by most of our customers. Your guests at home will welcome it on a hot day or as part of a casual party. Sasa prefers gazpacho with a bit more body, and he grumbles a little about this one. The secret to its great taste is to adjust the red wine vinegar judiciously at the end. Don't be shy. Add some, taste, add more, taste again—until it's right. Aside from its fresh flavors, the fact that this soup keeps for up to three days makes it perfect for a party.

Serves 4 to 6

Soup

3 pounds very ripe tomatoes, cored and chopped

2 red bell peppers, seeded, cored, and coarsely chopped

1 English cucumber, peeled and coarsely chopped

½ cup extra-virgin olive oil

6 cloves garlic, coarsely chopped

½ day-old round loaf Italian bread, crust removed and bread cut into 1-inch cubes (about 4 cups)

¼ cup sherry vinegar, or more to taste

1 teaspoon ground cumin

¼ teaspoon cayenne

½ teaspoon kosher salt, or more to taste

Freshly ground black pepper

4 cups tomato juice

Garnish

¼ day-old round loaf Italian bread, crust removed and bread cut into ½-inch cubes (about 2 cups)

¾ cup extra-virgin olive oil, plus about 2 tablespoons for drizzling

4 scallions, both white and green parts, thinly sliced

1 red bell pepper, seeded, cored, and cut into ½-inch dice

1 green bell pepper, seeded, cored, and cut into ½-inch dice

½ English cucumber, seeded and cut into ½-inch dice

1. To make the soup: In a large mixing bowl, combine the tomatoes, peppers, and cucumber.

2. In a sauté pan, heat the olive oil and garlic over medium heat and bring to a simmer. Simmer very gently for about 15 minutes, or until the garlic is browned and tender. Transfer to the mixing bowl and add the bread cubes.

3. Stir the ingredients together and then add the vinegar, cumin, cayenne, and salt. Season with black pepper and set aside for about 1 hour to marinate.

4. Working in batches, blend the marinated vegetable and bread mixture in a blender or a food processor fitted with the metal blade until pureed. Transfer the puree to a large bowl and continue until it is all pureed. If it is too dry, add a few tablespoons of tomato juice to thin it out to suit your taste.

5. Strain into another bowl and then stir in the tomato juice. Taste the soup and adjust the seasonings with salt and vinegar if needed. Cover and refrigerate for at least 3 hours or refrigerate in a container with a tight-fitting lid for up to 3 days.

6. For the garnish: Preheat the oven to 425°F.

7. Put the bread cubes in a medium bowl and pour the olive oil over them. Toss to mix so that the bread absorbs the olive oil and then spread the bread cubes in a single layer on a jelly-roll or similar baking pan and bake for about 4 minutes. Rotate the pan, turn the croutons over, and continue baking for about 4 minutes longer, or until they are golden brown and crisp. When done, let the croutons cool on the baking sheet. These will keep in a tightly lidded container for up to 2 days.

8. Ladle 1½ to 2 cups of soup into each chilled soup bowl. Garnish each with about 1½ tablespoons of the scallions, peppers, and cucumber. Top with about 2 tablespoons of croutons and a drizzle of olive oil. Serve immediately.

Salmorejo: Cordoban Gazpacho

This is the textured, thicker gazpacho Sasa prefers. Be sure to use *pimentón de la vera*, authentic smoked paprika, for this recipe. It's sold in many supermarkets, specialty shops, and Spanish food stores. It makes a difference, although any high-quality smoked paprika, such as Hungarian paprika, works nicely.

Serves 4 to 6

3 red bell peppers, seeded, cored, and coarsely chopped

3 pounds ripe beefsteak tomatoes (3 to 4 tomatoes), cored and chopped

1 day-old round loaf Italian peasant bread, crust removed and bread cut into 1-inch cubes (about 6 cups)

1 red onion, coarsely chopped

1 clove garlic, coarsely chopped

3 cups tomato juice

1 teaspoon kosher salt, or more to taste

¾ cup sherry vinegar

½ cup extra-virgin olive oil, plus more for drizzling

2 teaspoons sweet smoked paprika (*pimentón de la vera dulce*)

1 teaspoon hot smoked paprika (*pimentón de le vera picante*)

¼ pound slab Serrano ham, for garnish

1. In a food processor fitted with the metal blade, process about a third of the peppers, tomatoes, bread cubes, onion, and garlic until nearly but not completely smooth. Add 1 cup of the tomato juice and pulse to mix. Transfer the soup to a large bowl. Continue with the rest of the vegetables, bread, and tomato juice. Season with salt.

2. Stir the vinegar and olive oil into the soup and then season with the paprikas. Taste and adjust the salt if necessary.

3. Pour the soup into a container with a tight-fitting lid and refrigerate for at least 1 hour or for up to 2 days.

4. Slice the ham into very thin strips about ⅛ inch wide and then cut the strips into small cubes.

5. Ladle the chilled soup into chilled soup bowls and garnish each with some ham. Drizzle with a little olive oil and serve.

Heirloom Tomato Salad

There are very few ways to spoil a tomato salad if you follow these three tips. Number one: Buy tomatoes locally and in season. Check the tomato by smelling it, but if the stem is attached, don't smell the stem end. It's a trick of the trade to leave the stems on because they make the tomatoes smell better. Number two: Never buy a tomato if it feels cold and never refrigerate tomatoes. The cold kills their flavor. Number three: Apply small, judicious amounts of salt at the last possible moment, the coarser the better.

Serves 4

4 assorted ripe heirloom tomatoes, such as
Green Zebra, Brandywine, and Yellow Beefsteak,
cored and cut into ¼-inch-thick slices

5 fresh basil leaves, thinly sliced

¼ bunch fresh chives, chopped (2 to 3 tablespoons)

6 tablespoons extra-virgin olive oil

1 tablespoon aged balsamic vinegar

Kosher salt

Sea salt, for garnish

1. Overlap different-colored slices of tomato on a serving platter.

2. Sprinkle with the basil and chives. Drizzle the olive oil and vinegar over the tomatoes and season to taste with kosher salt.

3. Garnish with a little sea salt and serve.

Spicy Lobster Salad

People do love their lobster. Any way we serve it, it is a big hit. The strong flavors in this salad mean you can just put a little bit on a chip and still enjoy it. A single lobster will make enough for thirty or more chips.

Serves 4

One 1¼-pound live Maine lobster

2 ribs celery, cut into ¼-inch dice

2 tablespoons finely diced red onion

5 fresh chives, minced

½ jalapeño pepper, seeded, cored, and finely diced

1 teaspoon freshly squeezed lemon juice

Leaves from 4 sprigs fresh flat-leaf parsley, finely chopped

Leaves from 4 sprigs fresh dill, finely chopped

3 tablespoons sour cream

Cayenne

Pinch of kosher salt

About 30 potato chips or Yuca Chips (page 35) or 4 rounded Bibb lettuce leaves

1. In a large pot, bring about a gallon of water to a rolling boil over high heat. Put the lobster in the boiling water, head first, cover the pot, and cook for about 8 minutes, or until the lobster shell turns bright red.

2. Set a large bowl filled with ice and water next to the pot and, when the lobster is cooked, immediately plunge it into the ice water for about 15 minutes to cool.

3. When cool, remove the lobster meat from the claws, arms, and tail. Chop the meat into small bite-sized pieces and set aside.

4. In a large mixing bowl, toss together the celery, onion, chives, jalapeño, lemon juice, parsley, and dill. Add the lobster meat, sour cream, and cayenne to taste (we suggest starting with about ½ teaspoon) and mix well. Season to taste with salt and mix again.

5. Serve the lobster salad on chips or in the Bibb lettuce cups.

Chicken Liver Pâté

Pâté is a little time consuming to make but a breeze to serve, so it has an important place on the menu. We have a certain number of dishes that are ready-to-go so that the kitchen doesn't get bogged down. The same principle holds true for a dinner party. It's best to have a few things that you don't spend time on when guests are there. It's worth the investment in a nice terrine or another kind of attractive loaf pan for presentation at your party. Pâté can be made up to five days ahead, which is a boon for a harried host.

Serves 8 to 10

Pâté

3 tablespoons milk

2½ cups panko (Japanese bread crumbs)

2 pounds chicken livers, cleaned and patted dry

Kosher salt and freshly ground black pepper

4 teaspoons olive oil

5 shallots, thinly sliced

¼ cup brandy

½ pound slab bacon, well chilled or even semifrozen, rind removed and bacon cut into ¼-inch dice

3 cups water

½ pound ground pork

1 large egg

½ bunch fresh thyme, stems removed and leaves chopped

Pinch of ground cloves

Pinch of freshly grated nutmeg

Garnishes

Coarse Dijon mustard

Pickled onions

Capeberries

Endive spears

Radishes

Cornichons

Toasted baguette slices

1.   Position an oven rack in the middle of the oven. Preheat the oven to 375°F. Spray an 8 by 5 by 3-inch loaf pan with vegetable oil spray. Be sure the corners are well coated.

2.   In a small bowl, drizzle the milk over the bread crumbs, mix well, and set aside for no longer than 5 minutes to soften.

3.   Lightly season the chicken livers with salt and pepper.

4.   Heat a sauté pan over high heat and, when hot, pour 2 teaspoons of the olive oil into the pan and let it heat until very hot. Working in batches, sear the livers on all sides for about 2 minutes per side so that they are nicely browned but still pink in the center. As they sear, transfer the livers to a plate and let them cool in a single layer.

5.   Add the remaining 2 teaspoons of olive oil to the pan and sauté the shallots over medium-high heat for 4 to 5 minutes, or until translucent. Lift the pan from the heat and add the brandy. Hold the pan well away from you as the brandy may ignite.

6.   Return the pan to the heat and, using a wooden spoon, scrape up any browned bits stuck to the bottom of the pan. Pour the brandy and shallots from the pan into a small bowl and set aside.

7.   Add the bacon and water and bring to a boil over high heat. Cook for 8 to 10 minutes, or until the water evaporates. Reduce the heat to medium and let the bacon cook for about 5 minutes, or until the fat is rendered but the bacon is not necessarily browned.

8. In a food processor fitted with the metal blade, pulse the chicken livers and the shallots until coarsely chopped. Transfer to a large mixing bowl and add the bacon, ground pork, and bread crumbs. Add the egg and, using your hands, mix well.

9. Add the thyme, cloves, nutmeg, 1 teaspoon salt, and ¼ teaspoon pepper and mix well. Transfer to the loaf pan and smooth the top, gently pushing the mixture into the corners of the pan so that it fits snugly. Cover with aluminum foil.

10. Set the loaf pan in a larger roasting pan and put in the oven. Pour hot water into the roasting pan to come about halfway up the sides of the loaf pan. Bake for about 50 minutes, checking the pan every so often and adding water if it evaporates. The pâté is done when it feels firm and springy and a thermometer registers 140°F when inserted in the center.

11. Lift the loaf pan from the roasting pan and remove the aluminum foil. Set aside to cool for 1 to 1½ hours.

12. Run a sharp knife around the edges of the loaf pan and invert it onto a plate. Tap the top of the pan with the handle of a knife and, holding both the plate and the loaf pan, shake the two up and down to release the pâté.

13. Let the pâté cool completely and then wrap it well in plastic wrap and refrigerate for at least 2 hours and up to 5 days.

14. Serve garnished with Dijon mustard, pickled onions, caperberries, endive spears, radishes, and cornichons. Alternatively, slice the pâté into ¼-inch-thick slices about 2 inches long and serve on toasted baguette slices with a little coarse Dijon mustard.

OLIVE OIL

In keeping with our roots, we use only Spanish olive oil at our restaurants. When we opened, we went for the best-tasting oil we could find, and it often was Italian, but since then we have discovered plenty of great Spanish brands.

The olive oil has to taste great, feel smooth and rich in the mouth, and have a floral or fruity aroma. At the tables, we serve an extra-virgin oil with a full flavor profile, good ratio of fat to acid, and a nice balance of fruit and color. We pour this to eat with our bread, and our customers frequently ask us for the brand name of the oil. Truth is, we rarely stick with one brand for too long. Instead, we keep trying new ones, weighing one against the other as vintages change. We even hold olive oil tastings with the chefs and managers to make sure we are always pouring the best money can buy.

In the kitchens we use blended olive oil because its flavor is milder and it has a higher smoke point. This is why in many of our recipes we call for sautéing in "olive oil." This means you don't have to use the extra-virgin on the shelf but can instead use a less expensive olive oil. When we finish a dish with a pour of olive oil, we use extra-virgin.

Deciding on your own "house brand" of olive oil is fun. Buy several and try them to discover which you prefer. A lot of home cooks rely exclusively on extra-virgin olive oil, and this is fine, but the blended oils and those labeled "pure" are better for cooking.

Grilled Octopus Salad with White Beans

Octopus is a mainstay of all Mediterranean countries, and this is a nice way to eat it buffet style. Cooking the beans and the octopus takes a while, so it is best to do them the day before you plan to serve the octopus. You can buy good Spanish white beans, already cooked and packed in jars at specialty food stores, but they are also easy to prepare yourself.

Serves 6

½ pound dried giant Peruvian beans or other large dried white beans

3 quarts water

2 bay leaves

1 tablespoon black peppercorns

1 cooked octopus (see page 112)

3 ribs celery, thinly sliced on the diagonal

½ red onion, very thinly sliced (preferaby with a mandoline)

½ pint cherry tomatoes, halved

Juice of ½ lemon

5 teaspoons extra-virgin olive oil, plus a little for the octopus

Tabasco or other hot pepper sauce

Kosher salt and freshly ground black pepper

1. In a large pot, cover the beans with the water and add the bay leaves and peppercorns. Wrap the peppercorns in a cheesecloth bundle to make them easy to remove later. Bring to a boil over high heat, reduce the heat, and simmer for about 2 hours, or until the beans are tender but not mushy. The beans must be whole. Adjust the heat up or down to maintain the simmer. Skim any foam that rises to the surface of the pot.

2. Drain the beans, remove the bay leaves and peppercorns, and let the beans cool in the pot.

3. Prepare a charcoal or gas grill so that the charcoal or heating element is medium-hot. Before putting the grates on the grill, lightly spray them with flavorless vegetable oil spray.

4. Separate the legs from the body of the octopus and cut each leg into 4-inch-long sections. Discard the body. Cut each leg section in half horizontally.

5. Put the celery, onion, and tomatoes in a mixing bowl and dress with the lemon juice, 2 teaspoons of olive oil, and 4 dashes of Tabasco. Season to taste with salt and pepper and add more Tabasco if desired.

6. Lightly oil the octopus sections with the remaining 3 teaspoons of olive oil and lightly season with salt and pepper. Put the octopus, cut sides down, on the grill.

7. Grill for about 4 minutes, or until the octopus develops good color. Turn and grill for 2 to 3 minutes longer, or until cooked through with good color. Transfer the grilled octopus to the bowl with the vegetables and toss to mix.

8. Divide the vegetables among 6 serving plates, mounding them in the center. Toss the octopus pieces in any of the accumulated dressing left in the bowl and then divide them among the plates. Drizzle any leftover dressing over the plates and serve.

Marinated Eggplant with Red Pepper

This is a "scoop and serve" cold tapa that takes time to prepare but no time to serve. It belongs on a table full of interesting salads to accompany a meal or as one of a selection of dishes for a creative lunch. Try to buy "male" eggplants for fewer seeds. Males have a linear blemish on the end, whereas "females" have a round dot. We love this salad, partly because it can be made two days ahead of serving and refrigerated, which makes it great for entertaining.

Serves 6

2 large eggplants

2 tablespoons olive oil

2 red bell peppers

3 cloves garlic, chopped

3 tablespoons finely sliced fresh mint leaves

1 tablespoon sherry vinegar

2 teaspoons extra-virgin olive oil, plus more for drizzling

Kosher salt and freshly ground black pepper

Baguette slices, for serving

1. Preheat the oven to 450°F.

2. Rub the eggplants with olive oil, put in a shallow baking pan, and roast for 10 minutes. Turn the eggplants over and roast for 10 to 15 minutes longer, or until tender when pierced with a small knife. Let the eggplants cool.

3. Put the red peppers on the same pan and toss with a little olive oil. Roast for about 8 minutes, turn, and continue to roast for 8 to 10 minutes longer, or until the pepper flesh is tender and the skin is wrinkled and charred. Transfer the peppers to a medium bowl, cover with plastic wrap, and set aside to cool.

4. Cut the stem ends off the eggplants and then tear them open to separate the meat from the skins. Scrape out the seeds and shred the eggplant meat into strips about ½ inch thick. Transfer to a mixing bowl and add the garlic and mint.

5. Rub the skin from the peppers and then slice them open. Scrape out the seeds and membranes and slice about ⅛ inch thick. Add to the eggplant.

6. Sprinkle the vinegar and extra-virgin olive oil over the eggplant and toss to mix. Cover and refrigerate for at least 1 hour, or until chilled.

7. Bring the salad to room temperature, taste, and adjust the vinegar, salt, and pepper if necessary. Serve the salad on small plates, drizzled with a little more extra-virgin olive oil. Serve with the bread.

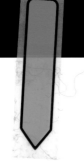

Roasted Chickpea Puree with Cumin-Toasted Pita Chips

The key to this dish is to get the consistency of the puree right—it should be closer to cream of wheat than spackle. Add water at the end if necessary.

Serves 4 to 6

Two 15-ounce cans
chickpeas, drained

6 scallions, both white and green
parts, coarsely chopped

4 shallots, coarsely chopped

1 bunch cilantro, thick
stems removed, leaves and
some stems chopped

¾ cup heavy cream

⅓ cup tahini

3 teaspoons ground cumin

½ teaspoon salt, or more to taste

1 lemon

½ cup water

Cumin-Toasted Pita Chips
(recipe follows)

¼ cup chopped scallion

1. Preheat the oven to 350°F.

2. On a jelly-roll or similar pan, spread the chickpeas in a single layer. You may need 2 pans. Sprinkle the coarsely chopped scallions, the shallots, and the cilantro over the chickpeas and roast for about 15 minutes, or until the chickpeas are dry and the scallions and cilantro darken.

3. Let the chickpeas cool in the pans. When cool, transfer the chickpeas, scallions, shallots, and cilantro to a food processor fitted with the metal blade. Add the heavy cream, tahini, cumin, and salt.

4. Heat the lemon in the microwave on high power for 15 seconds. Roll the lemon on the countertop under your palm to release the juices inside the lemon and then slice the lemon in half. Squeeze the juice from the lemon and then strain it into the food processor to remove its seeds.

5. Process the chickpea mixture until smooth. Do not overprocess. Taste and adjust the seasoning with salt if necessary. Scrape the puree from the food processor, set aside to cool to room temperature, and serve right away. If not ready to serve, put the puree in a container with a tight-fitting lid and refrigerate for up to 4 days. The puree can be served chilled or at room temperature.

6. When ready to serve, mound the chickpea puree in the center of a serving bowl. Arrange the chips in the puree by inserting their long sides into the base of the mound and then working upward. Garnish with the chopped scallion and serve.

cumin-toasted pita chips

This recipe comes from a friend's mother, who made these chips for cocktail parties. They are addictive and taste good with any sort of spread, such as the preceding Roasted Chickpea Puree. You will find dozens of other ways to serve them. Try them with salsa, hummus, or another dip.

Makes about 72 chips

One 12-ounce package pita bread with pockets

1¼ cups olive oil

½ cup ground cumin

2 tablespoons kosher salt

1. Preheat the oven to 425°F.

2. Slice each pita round in half and cut each half into 3 triangles for a total of 6 triangles. Separate each triangle into 2 halves and transfer to a large mixing bowl.

3. Drizzle the pita triangles with about ¾ cup of the olive oil and press the oil into the bread to saturate it. Season the triangles with the cumin and the salt. Rub the seasonings with one hand while tossing them with the other hand.

4. Spread the final ½ cup of olive oil over 2 jelly-roll or similar pans so that the oil covers them evenly and fully. Lay the pita triangles in an even layer on the pans.

5. Toast the chips for 12 to 14 minutes, or until honey brown and crisp. Turn with a spatula and rotate the pans several times to encourage even browning and crisping. Transfer the chips to racks to cool. Once cool, serve immediately or store in a container with a tight-fitting lid for up to 3 days.

Goat Cheese with Mojo Verde

This is a great dish to make ahead for parties as it keeps for as long as four days, although we admit it tastes best on the day it is made. It's flavorful, inexpensive, and exotic. When done right and allowed to sit at room temperature, the goat cheese softens so that it can be spread on toasted baguettes or crackers. After that, the brilliant green of the mojo verde starts to fade. It still tastes good the next day.

Serves 6

Goat Cheese Logs

6 sprigs fresh thyme

3 sprigs fresh flat-leaf parsley

2 sprigs fresh rosemary

¼ bunch fresh chives

Two 8-ounce logs goat cheese

¼ pound cream cheese

1 clove garlic, minced

Kosher salt and freshly
ground black pepper

Mojo Verde

1 green bell pepper, seeded,
cored, and cut into ¼-inch dice

¼ medium red onion, cut into
¼-inch dice (about ¼ cup)

¼ bunch fresh cilantro, stems
removed and leaves thinly sliced

1 clove garlic, minced

1 jalapeño pepper, cut into ¼-inch
dice (for less heat, scrape out the
seeds and membranes first)

2 tablespoons sherry vinegar

2 tablespoons extra-virgin olive oil

Juice of ½ lime

Kosher salt and freshly
ground black pepper

Baguette slices, flat bread, or
endive spears, for serving

1. To make the goat cheese logs: Strip the leaves from the thyme, parsley, and rosemary sprigs, discard the stems, and mince the leaves and the chives.

2. In an electric mixer fitted with the dough hook or the paddle attachment and set on medium speed, combine the goat cheese, cream cheese, garlic, and minced herbs. Season lightly with salt and pepper and mix well. Taste and adjust the seasonings.

3. Lay a sheet of plastic wrap about 1 foot long on a work surface. Using a rubber spatula, scrape enough of the cheese mixture along the plastic wrap to make a strip about 6 inches long and 1 inch wide. Roll the plastic wrap around the cheese to form a log about 6 inches long. Pinch and twist the ends to seal.

4. Continue to make logs with the cheese mixture until you have used all the mixture. You should have 2 to 3 logs. Refrigerate the logs for at least 2 hours and for up to 4 days.

5. To make the mojo verde: In a mixing bowl, mix together the bell pepper, onion, cilantro, garlic, and jalapeño. Add the vinegar, olive oil, and lime juice and mix gently. Season lightly with salt and pepper and stir well.

6. Using dental floss or a small, very sharp knife, slice the goat cheese logs into 18 rounds, each about ½ inch thick. Arrange 3 rounds on each of 6 serving plates to form a triangle. Spoon 2 tablespoons of the mojo verde on top of each round of cheese. The tapas can be prepared up to this point and left at room temperature for up to 2 hours or refrigerated for up to 6 hours. Let them return to room temperature before serving.

7. Serve with the baguette, flat bread, or endive spears.

Avocado Salad with Hearts of Palm and Marinated Roasted Red Peppers

Hearts of palm are a very Spanish ingredient. They are most commonly sold in cans and so taste quite uniform. At their best, they are revelatory: crunchy, refreshing, woody, and almost citrusy.

We serve this salad in the winter, since the ingredients are all available and customers like it on gray days. It is more filling than most salads and can be made as a meal. The best way to take the pit out of an avocado is to embed the blade of a sharp knife carefully into it with a soft whack, and then turn the knife 90 degrees to loosen the pit.

Serves 4 to 6

Vinaigrette

1¼ cups olive oil

¼ cup sherry vinegar

3 tablespoons Dijon mustard

½ cup sliced shallot

Kosher salt and freshly
ground black pepper

Salad

4 red bell peppers or one 12-ounce
jar roasted red peppers, drained

2 tablespoons olive oil

2 scallions, both white and
green parts, thinly sliced

1 cup lightly packed, coarsely
chopped cilantro leaves

1 tablespoon sherry vinegar

1 teaspoon sweet smoked paprika
(*pimentón de la vera dulce*)

Cayenne

Kosher salt and freshly
ground black pepper

2 ripe avocados

One 14-ounce can hearts
of palm, drained

Extra-virgin olive oil, for garnish

Sea salt, for garnish

1. To make the vinaigrette: In a blender, combine the olive oil, vinegar, mustard, and shallot. Blend until pureed. Taste and season with salt and pepper. Set aside until ready to use or transfer to a lidded container and refrigerate for up to 5 days.

2. To make the red pepper salad: Preheat the oven to 450°F.

3. Rub the peppers with the olive oil. Lay the peppers on a baking sheet and roast for 12 to 15 minutes, or until the side of the peppers resting on the baking sheet is wrinkled and almost black. Turn the peppers over and continue roasting for 7 to 8 minutes longer, or until the peppers are nicely charred on all sides.

4. Transfer the peppers to a large bowl and cover with plastic wrap. Let the peppers steam as they cool in the bowl for about 10 minutes.

5. Lay the peppers on a work surface and scrape out the seeds and membranes. Slice the peppers into ¼-inch strips, transfer to a mixing bowl, and add the scallions and cilantro.

6. Sprinkle the peppers with the vinegar and paprika and cayenne to taste. Season to taste with salt and pepper. The peppers can be made to this point and refrigerated for up to 3 days.

7.   Slice the avocado in half lengthwise. Remove the pit and, using a large spoon, gently and carefully lift the avocado from the peel. Put the avocado halves cut sides down on a cutting board and make 5 or 6 lengthwise slices into the avocado from the fat end, being careful not to cut all the way to the tip of the fruit. This should leave the halves attached at one end.

8.   Slice the hearts of palm into rounds.

9.   Spoon about 2 tablespoons of the vinaigrette into the center of each of 4 to 6 salad plates. Using a knife as a spatula, gently lift the avocado halves from the cutting board and put it on one side of the plate. Gently press on the avocado halves with your hand to fan them out on the plates.

10. Put about ½ cup of the sliced hearts of palm in the center of the plate on top of the vinaigrette and about ½ cup of pepper salad on the side opposite the avocado. Garnish each plate with a drizzling of olive oil and some sea salt.

TAPAS PARTIES

When you make tapas at home for a party, you probably won't serve more than four or five different ones at once. Take a cue from us and use your most eclectic plates and small bowls. This is part of the fun. Mix and match meat, vegetable, and fish tapas so that you and your guests have a variety to sample. Make one deep-fried tapa and then give yourself a break and choose others that are easier to cook. Some cold tapas can be prepared ahead of time, and buying Spanish cured meats, full-flavored cheeses, and green and black olives makes for much less work when you are pressed for time.

As one batch of tapas gets devoured, you can cook the next. Invite guests into the kitchen to help you prep and cook them. Tapas parties are nothing if not informal, and experimenting with different flavors and seeing who likes what is part of the fun. Pour some great Spanish wine, turn up the volume of the music, set the tapas out on a large table, and let your guests help themselves.

tapas party for 6 to 8

Roasted Olives (page 29)

Roasted Beets with Cabrales and Toasted Walnuts
(page 31)

Filet Mignon with Horseradish Cream on Toasted Ficelle
(page 33)

Goat Cheese with Mojo Verde (page 56)

Bonito del Norte (page 64)

Morcilla Sausage with Caramelized Onions (page 115)

Red Sangria (page 4)

Blood Orange Margarita (page 16)

tapas party for 15 to 20

Tuna Tartare with Yuca Chips (page 34)

Citrus Seviche (page 36)

Pickled Green Pepper, Anchovy,
and Olive Spears "Gilda" (page 63)

Marinated Eggplant with Red Pepper (page 53)

Wild Mushrooms with Herbed Cheese (page 90)

Empanadas with Smoked Pepper Sauce (page 98)

Crab Cakes (page 97)

Gambas al Ajillo (page 80)

White Sangria (page 5)

Mojito (page 23)

Martini Manzana Roja (page 24)

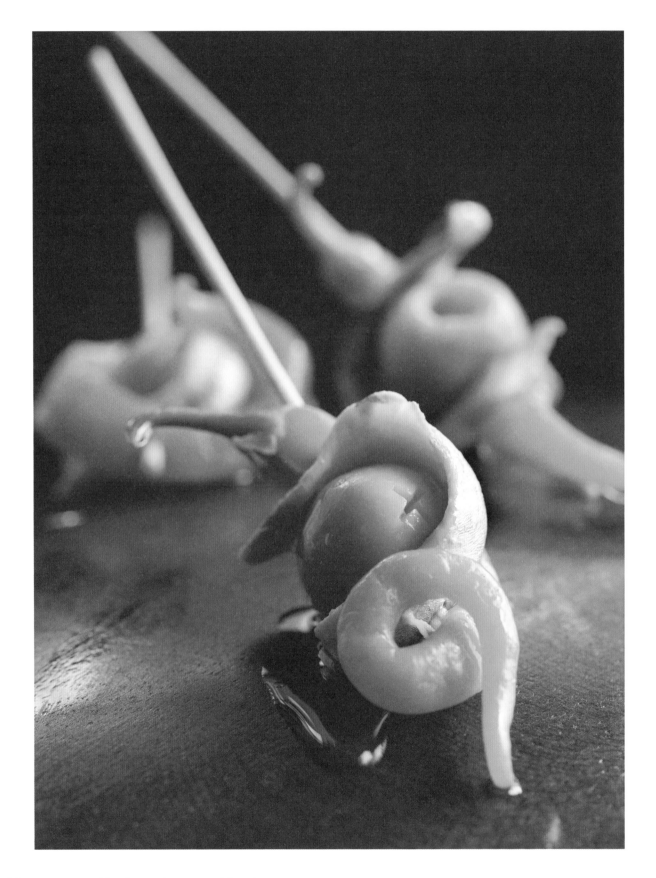

the barcelona cookbook

Pickled Green Pepper, Anchovy, and Olive Spears "Gilda"

This classic Basque tapa is served at every bar and tavern in San Sebastian and Bilbao. It is named for the famous Rita Hayworth film, which is set in Buenos Aires and much admired by the Spanish Basques. This is a flexible tapa; you can substitute small, sweetly sour cornichon pickles for the pickled peppers. Cornichons (*cornichon* means "gherkin" in French) are sold just about anywhere that sells pickles and olives. As you eat this tapa, the complex flavors surprise the mouth, and as delicious as it is, the parts are even better as a garnish for a dry martini.

Serves 6

300 grams (about 10½ ounces) canned high-quality salt-packed anchovy fillets or imported vinegar-packed *boquerones*, well rinsed and patted dry

One 12¼-ounce can imported pitted Spanish green olives, drained

One 4½-ounce jar *guindillas vascas* (pickled peppers) or peperoncini, drained and stemmed

Twenty-four ¼-inch-thick slices baguette

1.   Thread 1 anchovy on a sturdy toothpick or 3-inch bamboo skewer by piercing it at one end. Push an olive onto the toothpick and then run the other end of the anchovy over the olive and pierce near the center.

2.   Push a pepper onto the toothpick and run the end of the anchovy over the pepper, piercing it at its end. Repeat with 23 more toothpicks, using 1 anchovy, 1 olive, and 1 pepper for each.

3.   Mound the skewers decoratively on a serving plate. Serve immediately with baguette slices or cover and refrigerate for up to 24 hours.

Bonito del Norte

American tuna is generally albacore—an inexpensive, white-fleshed fish rarely sold except boiled in a can. In Spain (and Italy for that matter), they process the very best tuna, and the product in the cans is a delicacy, and so we recommend you look for imported tuna, which is surprisingly easy to find in most supermarkets. Try to keep this light and fluffy—don't overmix. This is a great lunch salad or a light, healthful dinner.

Piquillo peppers are hand-picked and roasted over open fires in northern Spain before being packed in jars or cans. They are small and red and tend to be sweet rather than sharp. Their nicely balanced flavor enhances any number of dishes.

Serves 4

Two 6-ounce cans highest-quality oil-packed Spanish or Italian tuna, such as Bonito del Norte, well drained

3 piquillo peppers, drained

2 scallions, both white and green parts, thinly sliced

Leaves from 6 sprigs fresh flat-leaf parsley, slivered

2 teaspoons drained capers

Finely sliced zest and juice of ½ lemon

Kosher salt and freshly ground black pepper

4 cups mesclun or baby arugula leaves

2 hard-cooked eggs, chopped

¼ cup Barcelona Aïoli (recipe follows)

1. Put the tuna in a medium mixing bowl and flake with a fork.

2. Slice the peppers into ⅛-inch-thick strips and add to the mixing bowl. Add the scallions, parsley, capers, and lemon zest and juice. Stir to mix and season to taste with salt and pepper.

3. Cover the bowl and refrigerate for at least 1 hour or for up to 24 hours.

4. Put 1 cup of mesclun on each of 4 serving plates or put all the greens in a large serving bowl.

5. Drain the mixture tuna of any accumulated juices and put about ½ cup of the tuna in a 4-inch ring mold set on top of the greens on each serving plate. Lift the ring off the packed tuna and repeat to make 4 servings. Alternatively, use an ice-cream scoop to mound the tuna on the greens if serving family style.

6. Top the tuna with chopped egg and then add a dollop of aïoli on top of the egg and serve.

barcelona aïoli   Poached garlic makes this a very mild aïoli. If you like a real garlic punch, replace a few of the poached cloves with raw ones. If the finished product is a tad lackluster, add more lemon juice.

Makes about 1¼ cups

6 cloves garlic

½ cup plus 1 tablespoon extra-virgin olive oil

1 cup mayonnaise

Juice of ½ lemon

Kosher salt and freshly ground black pepper

1.   In a small saucepan, combine the garlic cloves and ½ cup of the olive oil and bring to a simmer over medium heat. Cook for 5 to 7 minutes, or until the garlic is tender and honey gold. Watch the garlic carefully so that it does not overcook. Lift the garlic cloves from the oil with a slotted spoon and set aside on paper towels to cool. Discard the oil.

2.   In a food processor fitted with the metal blade, puree the garlic cloves, mayonnaise, lemon juice, and remaining tablespoon of olive oil until smooth. Taste, season with salt and pepper, and pulse to mix.

3.   Scrape the aïoli into a lidded storage container and chill for up to 3 days.

Fire-Roasted Peppers with Boquerones

These are two very typical Spanish ingredients turned into a canapé. Imported from Spain, *boquerones* are thin fillets of high-quality white anchovies packed in vinegar and salt or a combination of Spanish olive oil, vinegar, and salt. When you get the *boquerones*, drain them well and repack them in a jar, covered with high-quality olive oil and fresh parsley. They'll keep for a few weeks and certainly until you are ready to assemble the tapas.

Serves 4

48 pieces drained *boquerones*

1¾ cups extra-virgin olive oil

2 cloves garlic, very thinly sliced (preferably using a mandoline)

2 red bell peppers

4 scallions, both white and green parts, thinly sliced on the diagonal

¼ teaspoon sweet smoked paprika (*pimentón de la vera dulce*)

Kosher salt

Twelve ½-inch-thick baguette slices

1. In a medium glass or ceramic bowl, mix together the *boquerones*, 1 cup of the olive oil, and the garlic slices. Toss well, cover, and refrigerate for at least 2 hours and up to 2 days.

2. Preheat the oven to 450°F.

3. Rub the peppers with 1 tablespoon of the remaining olive oil. Lay the peppers on a baking sheet and roast for 12 to 15 minutes, or until the side of the peppers resting on the baking sheet is wrinkled and almost black. Turn the peppers over and continue roasting for 7 to 8 minutes longer, or until the peppers are nicely charred on all sides.

4. Transfer the peppers to a medium bowl and cover with plastic wrap. Let the peppers steam as they cool in the bowl for about 10 minutes.

5. Pull the charred skin from the peppers and cut each one in half. Remove the membranes and scrape out the seeds. Slice the peppers into strips about ⅛ inch wide and transfer to the bowl with the *boquerones*.

6. In another small bowl, combine the scallions with about 3 tablespoons of the remaining olive oil. Season with the paprika and a pinch of salt. Set aside until needed or cover and refrigerate for up to 24 hours.

7. Preheat the oven to 425°F.

8. Drizzle the remaining ½ cup of olive oil on both sides of the baguette slices and lay the slices on a baking sheet. Toast for 5 to 6 minutes, or until lightly browned. Rotate the baking sheet and turn the bread slices over. Toast for about 5 minutes longer, or until crispy and honey brown.

9. Let the bread slices cool and then top each with about 2 tablespoons of the pepper mixture. Lay 3 *boquerones* on top of the peppers and serve.

OUR TRIPS TO SPAIN

We started taking groups of our chefs and managers to Spain to explore the wineries, markets, cafés, bars, and restaurants. This way, our staff soaks up the culture and history of the countryside and the cities and is inspired to make our menu even more authentic. They can experience firsthand the mood of the restaurants, the seasonality of the food, and the way restaurants in Spain are integrated into daily life rather than being seen as special-occasion places. We focus our visits on different regions, almost always including the wine regions, also known as DOs ("designations of origin"). Our business contacts in Spain help us plan these trips so they are as exciting as possible. For example, José Luis Ripa, a small wine producer and culinary enthusiast, has orchestrated some of our most memorable tours of the DOs of Rioja and Cigales. He guided us through the monumental Museum Real winery and took us for an impromptu visit with the president of the DO of Cigales—the man in charge of all the winemaking in the region.

We have fond memories, too, of the spectacular Baron de Ley Winery in Logroño, where we were presented with a multicourse feast that showcased the spring harvest of Rioja. The winery is housed in an old monastery, which still has a sanctified chapel. Spring was in full bloom, and the grapevines were bursting with new leaves. José guided us through the monastery so we could explore every nook of the old building and touch stone that had seen hundreds of years. We ate and drank like kings and at the end of the afternoon were presented with certificates, which we had a hard time reading as the words kept moving.

Victor Solorca is another friend who has shown us endless hospitality. On a recent trip he took the time to expose us to the surprising complexity of the rustic, cuisine of Ribera del Duero. Among hectares of ripening grapevines, Victor has built a modern, immaculate winery called Solorca with a stately marbled showroom. He prepared a meal of suckling lamb for us, grilling it over the embers of last year's grapevines.

Francisco Castro and José González Oliver, both of Giraldo, Spain's premier producer of bacalao (salt cod), are also unforgettable for their generosity and hospitality. Their fish-processing facility is modern, sterile, and streamlined, and, interestingly enough, HAACAP certified (an American safety and quality standard), which is rare for a European producer.

Artisans such as these are the best local tour guides. They invited us to the best pintxos (tapas) bar in Vittoria and possibly in all of northern Spain. We spent a magical day with José driving the coastline near Bilbao and learned a number of tricks for making pintxos from him, which have turned up on our menus.

Mussels on the Half Shell with Escabeche

Escabeche is basically a pickle, or a sweet-and-sour way to preserve seafood, often with vegetables. This recipe, like all for escabeche, needs time to marinate, so allow at least four hours. You can also make this up to two days ahead of serving. Watch the mussels as they cook and be sure to remove them as they open so that they don't overcook. The dish is best served on a buffet with plates, as it can be a little messy to eat.

Serves 4

Escabeche

1 red bell pepper, cut into ⅛-inch dice

1 green bell pepper, cut into ⅛-inch dice

1 plum tomato, peeled and cut into ⅛-inch dice

1 red onion, cut into small dice

2 cloves garlic, crushed and then finely chopped

Leaves from 8 sprigs fresh thyme, finely chopped

¼ teaspoon sugar

1 cup extra-virgin olive oil

½ cup sherry vinegar

2 tablespoons red wine vinegar

Pinch of kosher salt

Mussels

24 Prince Edward Island mussels or other high-quality mussels

2 cups dry white wine

1. To prepare the escabeche: In a large mixing bowl, mix together the peppers, tomato, onion, garlic, thyme, and sugar. Add the olive oil and vinegars and stir gently to combine. Season with the salt. Cover and refrigerate for at least 4 hours or for up to 2 days.

2. To prepare the mussels: Clean the mussels by scrubbing well under cold running water and removing any beards. Drain well.

3. Heat a large sauté pan over high heat and, when hot, put the mussels in the pan with the wine. Cover and cook for 5 to 7 minutes, shaking the pan occasionally, until the mussels open. Lift the mussels from the pan as they open. (Discard any that do not open.)

4. Spread the mussels in a single layer in a shallow baking pan and, when they cool a little, refrigerate for about 1 hour, or until chilled.

5. Pull the top shells off the mussels and then, using your fingers, release and remove the mussel meat from the bottom shell. Remove and discard the connector muscle in the shell and then return the meat to the clean shells.

6. Arrange the mussels on a platter in a circular pattern and top each with about 1 tablespoon of escabeche. Or you can top the mussels with escabeche first and then arrange them. Serve immediately.

chapter 3

Hot Tapas

The ten top-selling dishes on our menu fall into this category. When you visit Barcelona on a busy night, the slide—which is the name for the part of the kitchen where the finished plates are put by the cooks to be picked up by waiters—is filled with hot tapas in every possible combination and served on a dozen differently sized and shaped plates.

The dishes in this chapter include some of the more complicated ones in the book. We recommend making a few and sharing them as a main course, rather than following them with an entrée. These dishes evolved over time with the input of some very talented chefs. This is the first time we have shared the recipes, and we hope you find them as appealing and intriguing as we do.

Let our recipes inspire you to invent your own hot tapas. Take the same approach we take: First, find whatever looks appealing to you at the produce market, on the meat counter, or at the fish market. Next, season it with salt and pepper, a little garlic, and some olive oil. Grill it or cook it in a pan for long enough to cook it through and then serve it immediately with lemon, olive oil, and some chopped fresh herbs. There's nothing complicated about it, and nothing better.

Mussels al Diablo

This is Sasa's dish, borrowed from a restaurant he worked in and—like many of our best-selling dishes—Italian through and through. This dish follows the Barcelona precept: simple preparation and big, striking flavors. We serve a large crouton with it, but people will typically go through an additional basket of bread to finish the broth.

Serves 4

40 Prince Edward Island mussels or other high-quality mussels

1 cup olive oil

¼ baguette, sliced on the diagonal into eight ¼-inch-thick pieces

2 tablespoons chopped garlic

2 cups canned tomatoes with their juice, crushed

1 teaspoon hot red pepper flakes

Kosher salt

1 cup dry white wine

½ bunch fresh flat-leaf parsley, stems removed and leaves slivered, plus more for garnish

2 tablespoons extra-virgin olive oil, for garnish

1. Preheat the oven to 425°F.

2. Clean the mussels by scrubbing well under cold running water and removing any beards. Drain well, transfer to a large bowl, and refrigerate.

3. Pour ½ cup of the olive oil into a shallow baking dish. Lay the bread slices in the oil and turn once to coat both sides. Toast the bread for 10 to 15 minutes, turning once or twice, or until golden brown and crisp. Transfer the croutons to a plate to cool.

4. Pour the remaining ½ cup of olive oil into a large sauté pan and heat over medium heat. Add the garlic and cook for 2 to 3 minutes, or until lightly browned. Add the mussels, tomatoes, and pepper flakes and season with salt to taste. Stir well and cook for about 15 minutes.

5. Add the wine and parsley, cover, and cook for about 3 minutes, or until all the mussels open. (Discard any that do not open.)

6. Pour the mussels and the sauce into a large serving bowl. Garnish with parsley and drizzle with extra-virgin olive oil. Stud the bowl with the croutons and serve.

Rabbit with Porcini Mushrooms and Red Wine

One reason people enjoy tapas is that they provide diners with the opportunity to explore, on a small scale, food they might not be willing to commit to as a main course. We love rabbit and try to offer it as a special on the menu on a regular basis.

When doing white-meat braises, like rabbit or chicken, it is very important to keep the heat as low as possible so the meat never boils in the stock. Fresh rabbit will give a much superior product to frozen, so give your butcher some advance notice and he should be able to get it for you. You may also want to ask him to prepare the rabbit for you, as described in step 1.

Serves 4

Rabbit

Two 3-pound rabbits

Kosher salt and freshly ground black pepper

2 cups all-purpose flour

3 tablespoons olive oil

1 large Spanish onion, sliced

1 clove garlic, crushed

2 ribs celery, chopped

1 carrot, peeled and chopped

3 cups dry red wine

2 cups chicken stock

6 sprigs fresh thyme

6 black peppercorns

2 bay leaves

Sauce

3 cups water

1 cup dried porcini mushrooms (4 to 5 ounces)

1 tablespoon olive oil

1 large Spanish onion, minced

Kosher salt

1 clove garlic, minced

2 ribs celery, minced

5 sprigs fresh thyme

Freshly ground black pepper

1. To prepare the rabbit: Use a sharp boning knife to remove the front and rear legs from the rabbit at the joints. Slice down the spines and through the backbones to separate the 2 back sections. Cut through the rib bones about 1½ inches from the bottom and separate into 2 sections. You can ask the butcher to do this for you.

2. Season the rabbit pieces with salt and pepper.

3. Spread the flour in a shallow dish and dredge the rabbit pieces in it.

4. In a deep sauté pan over medium heat, heat 2 tablespoons of the olive oil for about 1 minute. Working in batches, brown the rabbit pieces for 5 to 7 minutes on each side. Do not crowd the pan. Remove each piece from the pan when it turns honey brown.

5. Discard the oil, wipe out the pan with a paper towel, and return to medium-low heat. Add the remaining tablespoon of olive oil and sauté the onion for about 8 minutes, stirring frequently, until soft and translucent but without color. Add the garlic, celery, and carrot to the pan and cook gently for 8 to 10 minutes longer, or until the vegetables soften.

6.   Return the rabbit pieces to the pan and add the wine, stock, thyme, peppercorns, and bay leaves. Raise the heat to high and bring to a simmer. Reduce the heat to low, cover the pan with aluminum foil, and simmer gently for about 1½ hours. Adjust the heat up or down to maintain a low simmer. If the liquid evaporates, add enough water to cover the rabbit halfway and continue cooking.

7.   To prepare the sauce: In a saucepan, bring the water and mushrooms to a bare simmer over medium heat and cook for about 45 minutes, or until the mushrooms are tender and hydrated. Strain the mushrooms through a fine sieve, coffee filter, or double layer of cheesecloth and reserve the liquid. Chop the mushrooms and set aside.

8.   When the meat on the rear legs of the rabbit can easily be pulled from the bone, remove the rabbit pieces from the pan and set aside to cool.

9.   Strain the braising liquid through a fine-mesh sieve. Discard the vegetables and reserve the liquid.

10. Pull the meat from the leg bones and shred it with your hands. Run your fingers along the top of the backbones to release the loin meat. Shred this meat too.

11. In a deep sauté pan, heat the remaining tablespoon of olive oil and sauté the onion with a pinch of salt over low heat for 8 to 10 minutes, or until soft and translucent. The onion should not brown. Add the garlic, celery, and thyme and cook gently for about 10 minutes, or until soft.

12. Add the chopped mushrooms and the reserved braising liquid and mushroom liquid to the sauté pan. Raise the heat to high and boil for 15 to 20 minutes, until reduced by half.

13. Return the shredded meat to the sauté pan and continue cooking over low heat for 5 to 7 minutes longer, or until the mixture has a saucelike consistency and the rabbit is heated through.

14. Ladle the rabbit, vegetables, and sauce into 4 shallow bowls and serve.

Steak Paillard

In this dish we take the best New York strip steak (which we settled on after years of searching for the most successful cut) and cut it into thin steaks. We grill them perfectly and serve them with matchstick potatoes and a great light sauce. This isn't like getting a giant strip steak: it's a taste for much less money, and you still have room to try other things. Our mantra: you don't have to give up quality to spend less.

Serves 4

Vinaigrette

1 red bell pepper, finely diced

1 green bell pepper, finely diced

1 plum tomato, finely diced

1 red onion, finely diced

2 cloves garlic, diced

Leaves from 8 sprigs fresh thyme, chopped

1 cup extra-virgin olive oil

½ cup sherry vinegar

2 tablespoons red wine vinegar

Kosher salt and freshly ground black pepper

Steak and Potatoes

2 russet potatoes

7 cups canola or peanut oil, for deep frying

Kosher salt

Four 3-ounce New York strip steaks, pounded to a thickness of about ¼ inch

Freshly ground black pepper

½ teaspoon olive oil

1.   To prepare the vinaigrette: In a medium glass or ceramic mixing bowl, toss the bell peppers, tomato, onion, garlic, and thyme leaves.

2.   Add the olive oil and vinegars. Whisk well and season to taste with salt and pepper.

3.   To prepare the steak and potatoes: Peel the potatoes and cut into very thin strips, ⅛ to ¼ inch wide. (If you have a mandoline, use it.) Put the potatoes in a bowl filled with cold water to wash off any surface starch. Drain very well and pat dry.

4.   In a deep, heavy pot, heat the oil over high heat until a deep-fat thermometer reaches 375°F.

5.   Shake the colander to remove any excess water from the potatoes. Working in batches, drop 1 cup of potatoes into the hot oil. Stir them carefully with a long-handled slotted spoon and fry for 4 to 5 minutes, or until lightly browned and crisp. Lift the fried potatoes from the oil and drain on a

baking sheet lined with paper towels. Season the hot potatoes with salt.

6.   Let the oil regain its heat between batches. Repeat until all the potatoes are fried and salted.

7.   Lightly spray the grid of your gas or charcoal grill with flavorless vegetable oil spray. Preheat the gas grill or prepare the charcoal grill so that the heating element or charcoal is hot.

8.   Season the steaks on both sides with salt and pepper and then lightly oil them with olive oil. Grill for about 2 minutes on one side. Turn and grill for about 30 seconds longer for medium-rare meat. Alternately, you could cook the steaks in a very hot cast-iron skillet instead of the grill.

9.   Put 1 steak on each of 4 serving plates and spoon about 3 tablespoons of the vinaigrette on top of each. Put about ½ cup of fried potatoes next to the steak and serve.

Duck Confit with Oyster Mushrooms and Reduced Port

This dish came from Chef David Curtis many years ago and returns to the menu every November when the weather changes and we start looking for stews. You can make your own duck confit by cooking duck legs in a layer of duck or goose fat, slowly, for hours, and it produces a marginally better result, but there is excellent confit available in specialty stores.

Serves 4

6 confit duck legs

¼ cup olive oil

Two 10-ounce packages oyster mushrooms or other forest mushrooms, cleaned of woody bottoms and torn into pieces

Kosher salt

½ cup sliced shallots (6 to 7 shallots)

1½ cups reduced rich veal or beef stock (see Note)

¾ cup nonvintage port

2 teaspoons chopped fresh thyme leaves

1. Remove and discard the skin from the duck legs. Pull the meat from the bones, shred it, and set aside.

2. In a 9- or 10-inch sauté pan over medium-high heat, heat 2 tablespoons of the olive oil. Add the mushrooms and sear, without stirring, for about 5 minutes, or until they color. Add salt to taste.

3. Add the shallots and cook, stirring, for 3 to 4 minutes, or until they soften.

4. Add the stock and port and simmer rapidly for 15 to 20 minutes, or until slightly thickened with a saucelike consistency. Add the duck meat and the thyme, stir well to mix, and heat without boiling for 4 to 5 minutes.

5. Spoon the duck, mushrooms, and sauce into 4 shallow bowls and serve.

6. This dish can be made ahead of time and refrigerated in a tightly lidded container for up to 2 days. Reheat gently over medium heat or in the microwave.

Note: Rich, reduced veal stock is full flavored and adds a lot to this dish. You can buy it at some specialty stores or make your own by reducing a good stock for several hours. As it cooks down, the water evaporates and the flavor intensifies. Veal stock becomes particularly silken and viscous and results in glorious sauces; beef stock tastes stronger. If you buy commercial stock and reduce it, buy low-sodium stock because storebought ones tend to be salty. If you can, buy stock from a local shop that makes its own and reduce it yourself—or ask if they sell rich, reduced stock.

Gambas al Ajillo

This was our first tapa. *Gambas al Ajillo* means "shrimp with garlic," and there are as many ways to serve this combination as there are restaurants in Spain. Andy and Martha Hartley, our very first chef, worked on it and made dozens of versions before coming up with this one. Ours has sherry, thyme, and red pepper, and making it right is all about balance. New cooks tend to put in too much red pepper flakes, so we changed the recipe in the restaurant to use a single uncrushed guindilla pepper. The sherry is intimately tied to the balance, and luckily it's a brand that is easy to find in any American town. Most important, we use only top-quality white or pink South American shrimp or, when prices are reasonable, Gulf shrimp. Use the best you can buy.

Serves 4

20 medium shrimp (21–25 count), peeled and deveined, with tails left on

Kosher salt and freshly ground black pepper

2 teaspoons olive oil

4 cloves garlic, very thinly sliced (preferably with a mandoline)

1 cup Christian Brothers Golden Sherry

2 pinches of hot red pepper flakes

Leaves from 4 sprigs fresh thyme

1 tablespoon unsalted butter

1. Lightly rinse the shrimp under cool running water. Drain and pat dry with paper towels. Lightly season the shrimp with salt and pepper.

2. In a sauté pan, heat the olive oil over high heat. Add the garlic and shrimp and sear for about 3 minutes, turning once or twice, or until the garlic is lightly browned. Add the sherry to the pan, being careful in case it ignites (if it does, remove the pan from the heat and the flames will subside quickly). Stir in the pepper flakes and thyme and cook for a few minutes longer, or until the shrimp is cooked through and pink.

3. Using a slotted spoon, transfer the shrimp to a serving dish and leave the sherry in the pan. Still over high heat, reduce the sherry for 7 to 10 minutes, or until it becomes a glaze.

4. Add the butter to the pan, swirling it over medium heat until melted. Return the shrimp to the pan, toss with the glaze, and serve immediately.

OUR BREAD BASKET

When you serve as many tapas as we do, you need really good bread. We buy ours daily from a wholesale bakery located down the road from our Norwalk restaurant.

Spinelli Brothers makes only one kind of bread for wholesale distribution—a Tuscan loaf that we have been serving since we opened our doors. When it's delivered, it's not quite baked all the way through, so we finish the baking in our own ovens, which means it's essentially freshly baked when we carry it to the tables, swaddled in a big white napkin. Our customers go crazy for it. You won't find a recipe for our bread in the book, but we urge you to buy the best Italian-style loaf you can find. Some might call this sort of loaf "farmhouse" or "country-style," *panelle* or *ciabatta*. We call it fantastic.

Carmine and his brother Leo Spinelli run the business. Leo has been baking bread for thirty years, having learned the craft on Arthur Avenue, the famous boulevard in the Bronx with scores of authentic Italian markets, restaurants, butchers, delis, and bakeries. Carmine and his wife, Elise, like to come to the restaurant partly to bust Andy's chops. They pull aside a busboy or the waiter and say, "Hey, this bread is really good! Where do you get it?"

Sometimes Andy instructs the server to say, "We bake it here." Other times he tells the server to respond, "We buy it from the day-old section at the supermarket. Nobody really notices."

Once, when Andy saw Carm's name in the reservation book for later in the week, he lopped off a large piece of a fresh loaf and let it sit out for three days until it was as hard as a rock. When Carm and Elise and two other couples were seated, the busboy delivered the bread, wrapped as always in a bright white napkin. Even from a distance, Andy could see Carm gesture toward the bread basket and then try to tear off a piece. The look on his face as he attempted to hide the stale bread from his guests was worth every minute of planning.

Eggplant Rollatini

The first chef we hired at Barcelona to replace Andy was Bill Rosenberg from Port Chester, New York. Bill was an immensely talented chef who channeled nonexistent Italian roots in everything he did. He gave us some of our most enduring non-Spanish dishes; they were so good we just looked the other way or gave them Spanish names. We called this dish *berenjenas rellenas*, or stuffed eggplant, but really it's as Italian as it gets and uses capicola, a seasoned, dry-cured pork that, when very firm, is called *coppa*. Otherwise, it is similar to prosciutto, which is a good substitute. These are so delicious Andy used to eat them cold, with no sauce, when he found them in the walk-in.

Serves 6; makes about 18 rolls

Eggplant

2 cups all-purpose flour

1 teaspoon kosher salt

Freshly ground black pepper

3 large eggs

2 large firm eggplants

1 cup olive oil

Basil Puree

About 3 cups fresh basil leaves (from 2 large bunches)

1 clove garlic, lightly crushed

2 tablespoons extra-virgin olive oil

Tomato Sauce

2 tablespoons olive oil

1 large Spanish onion, thinly sliced

3 cloves garlic, coarsely chopped

One 35-ounce can Italian plum tomatoes

½ teaspoon kosher salt

Freshly ground black pepper

Leaves from 4 sprigs fresh basil, roughly torn

½ pound capicola, thinly sliced

½ pound provolone cheese, thinly sliced

1. To prepare the eggplant: Put the flour in a shallow bowl and season with ½ teaspoon of the salt and with pepper to taste. In another bowl, whisk the eggs with the remaining salt and a little pepper.

2. Peel the eggplants and then sliced lengthwise into ⅓-inch-thick slices. Dip each in the flour to coat both sides lightly. Dip the eggplant slice in the egg and then in the flour again. Set aside on a plate lined with paper towels until all the slices are coated.

3. Pour the oil into a shallow skillet or baking pan such as a jelly roll pan. You may need to use 2 pans, depending on the size, so that the eggplant slices are in a single layer. Set the pan(s) over medium heat on the stove for 3 to 4 minutes, or until hot. Carefully lay the eggplant slices in the pans and cook for about 7 minutes. Using tongs, turn the eggplant slices over and cook for about 4 minutes longer, or until tender and cooked through. Lift from the oil with tongs and drain on a paper towel–lined pan. (If desired, pack the cooled eggplant slices in an airtight container and refrigerate for up to 2 days.)

4. To make the basil puree: Put the basil leaves, garlic, and extra-virgin olive oil in a blender and puree until smooth. Use right away or refrigerate for up to 2 days.

5. To prepare the tomato sauce: Heat the olive oil in a large pot over medium heat. Add the onion and garlic and cook for about 10 minutes, or until softened but not colored. Add the tomatoes with their juice and crush them lightly with the back of a spoon while you bring them to a simmer. Season with the salt and with pepper to taste. Simmer for about 20 minutes, or until heated through.

6. Add the basil leaves and stir well.

7. Let the tomato sauce cool a little and then, working in batches, puree it in a blender until smooth. As one batch is pureed, transfer it to a bowl or a container with a tight-fitting lid. Use the tomato sauce right away or refrigerate for up to 3 days.

8. Preheat the oven to 400°F.

9. Spoon about half the tomato sauce over the bottom of a shallow casserole or gratin dish large enough to hold the eggplant rollatini in a single layer.

10. Lay the eggplant slices on a work surface and spread some basil puree on each one. Top each with 2 slices of capicola and a slice or two of provolone to make a single layer.

11. Starting at the narrow end of each eggplant slice, roll each to enclose the meat and cheese. Arrange seam side down in the casserole. Pack the rollatini snugly in the dish so that they support each other. Spoon the remaining tomato sauce over the eggplant.

12. Bake for 25 to 30 minutes, or until hot and bubbling.

THE CITY OF BARCELONA

Barcelona is our favorite city in Spain and one we never miss when we travel there. Once we arrive, we often make a beeline for La Cartes des Vins, near the Iglesia de Santa Maria del Mar, to speak with Gareth York. A British transplant to Catalonia, Gareth was a sous chef at Barcelona's Ritz before becoming a full-time oenophile. Born with the gift of the gab, he entertains us even as he steers us to restaurant landmarks such as Santa Maria, Commerce 24, Cal Pep, Moo, and Hoffman, among others.

This is a cosmopolitan city where you can dine in restaurants serving French, Turkish, or Japanese food, for example. This is true of most world-class cities, of course, but in Barcelona it is also possible to sample the glorious Catalan cuisine of the region, as served in the restaurants just mentioned.

As well as trying restaurants, we love to wander through Barcelona's famed outdoor food market, La Boquería, filled with stall after stall of local cheeses, glistening fish and seafood, cured hams, hanging chorizo sausages, freshly baked breads, and tempting fruits and vegetables. It's located just steps off Las Ramblas, Barcelona's most famous street, through latticed iron gates, and scattered throughout it are tapas bars, ideal for quick lunches.

Our visits to Barcelona and other cities in Spain have proven to be enriching on many levels. They have imbued us and our staff with a deep appreciation and passion for Spanish wine and food. Chance encounters with local businesspeople, diners at adjacent tables, and shopkeepers have enhanced our understanding of the culture and resulted in some rewarding friendships. The spirit of this generous and culinarily inspiring country is one we hope translates to our restaurants and our food.

Chorizo with Sweet-and-Sour Figs

After our chef Bill Rosenberg left in 1999, our next executive chef was David Curtis, who came from stints at some of the top Spanish restaurants in the United States. This dish is his invention. We are often asked by new customers examining the menu, "What is your most popular dish?" In terms of loyal adherents, this dish is probably as close to a "signature" as we have. It's simple and exciting at the same time. Andy's son asked him to send the recipe to him when he was away at school because he wanted to make something special for his friends. Chorizo is easy to find in many supermarkets, specialty stores, and Spanish markets, and dried figs are widely available.

Serves 4 to 6

1 tablespoon olive oil

2 pounds smoked Spanish chorizo, cut on the diagonal into slices about ¼ inch thick

3 cloves garlic, minced

2 cups dried white Turkish figs, stemmed and quartered

1¼ cups sherry vinegar

⅔ cup balsamic vinegar

1 cup packed dark brown sugar

1½ cups water

1½ teaspoons ground cinnamon

3 whole cloves

1. In a large sauté pan, heat the olive oil over medium high heat for about 1 minute. Working in batches, sear the chorizo and garlic for 2 to 3 minutes, turning the sausage once during cooking. Set the sausage aside.

2. Put the figs in a medium saucepan with the vinegars, brown sugar, water, cinnamon, and cloves. Bring to a simmer over medium heat and cook for about 10 minutes, adjusting the heat up or down to maintain the simmer.

3. Divide the chorizo among 6 bowls. Pour the figs and the pan sauce over the chorizo and serve piping hot.

Pan-Roasted Ostrich Fillet
with Brandy Reduction and Garlic Confit

This is another David Curtis dish. It is remarkably simple on the plate: just sliced ostrich, veal demi-glace, and garlic confit. Ostrich is not nearly as hard to find these days as when we first started using it, but it is still an object of fascination. Remember not to cook ostrich beyond medium-rare and to let it rest for several minutes before slicing it.

Serves 4

Garlic Confit	*Ostrich*	¾ cup brandy
12 cloves garlic	Two 6-ounce ostrich fillets	¾ cup heated veal stock
1 cup olive oil	Kosher salt and freshly ground black pepper	1 tablespoon unsalted butter

1. To prepare the confit: In a small saucepan over medium heat, heat the garlic cloves and olive oil to a simmer. Cook for about 12 minutes, or until the garlic cloves are tender and lightly browned. Adjust the heat up or down to maintain the simmer and watch the garlic carefully so that it does not burn.

2. Transfer the garlic and oil to a small bowl or rigid plastic container and let the oil cool a little. Cover and refrigerate for 2 to 3 hours, until chilled, and up to 3 days.

3. To prepare the ostrich: Preheat the oven to 475°F.

4. Season the ostrich fillets on both sides with salt and pepper.

5. Heat an ovenproof sauté pan over medium-high heat. Add 2 tablespoons of the olive oil from the confit to the pan and, when hot, sear the fillets on both sides until golden brown. Transfer the sauté pan to the oven and roast for about 6 minutes, or until medium-rare. Do not overcook. Let the fillets rest on a cutting board.

6. Put the garlic cloves from the confit in the sauté pan. Remove the pan from the heat and add the brandy. Return the pan to the heat and be mindful that the brandy might ignite. Cook the brandy for about 1 minute. Pour about two-thirds of the hot stock into the pan and cook for 4 to 5 minutes, or until the sauce thickens so that it coats the back of a spoon. Add more stock if the sauce gets too thick.

7. Swirl the butter into the sauce and adjust the seasoning.

8. Meanwhile, slice the ostrich fillets into 8 to 10 thin slices and fan 4 or 5 slices of meat on each of 4 plates. Garnish each plate with 3 cloves of garlic and spoon about 3 tablespoons of sauce over the ostrich.

Wild Mushrooms with Herbed Cheese

This is a flavor combination that Andy has always liked—wild mushrooms and balsamic vinegar. It's the way he used to prepare them at Stars in San Francisco, where they also used goat cheese as a counterpoint. At Barcelona, our original recipe used a piece of French goat cheese, but now we use an herbed, garlicked goat cheese mixture, which melts much better and more evenly. This dish perks up quickly in the microwave, so it's a great last-minute piece of a meal.

Serves 4

Herbed Cheese

Two 8-ounce logs goat cheese, at room temperature

¼ pound cream cheese, at room temperature

Leaves from 6 sprigs fresh thyme, minced

Leaves from 3 sprigs fresh flat-leaf parsley, minced

Leaves from 2 sprigs fresh rosemary, minced

¼ bunch fresh chives, minced

1 clove garlic, minced

Kosher salt and freshly ground black pepper

Mushrooms

3 tablespoons olive oil

10 ounces shiitake mushrooms, stemmed and sliced

10 ounces oyster mushrooms or other forest mushrooms, torn into ¼-inch pieces

10 ounces cremini mushrooms, all but ¼ inch of stems removed, sliced

¼ teaspoon kosher salt

Freshly ground black pepper

4 shallots, thinly sliced

1½ cups veal stock

3 tablespoons balsamic vinegar

2 tablespoons chopped fresh thyme

1. To prepare the cheese: In an electric mixer fitted with the paddle attachment and set on medium speed, mix together the goat cheese, cream cheese, thyme, parsley, rosemary, chives, and garlic for about 1 minute. Season to taste with salt and pepper and beat for 2 to 3 minutes longer or very well blended.

2. Spread a sheet of plastic wrap about 12 inches long on a work surface. Spread about half of the cheese mixture along the bottom third of the plastic wrap, leaving 1 inch on each end. Roll the plastic wrap around the cheese to make a log approximately 1 to 1½ inches in diameter. Twist the clean ends of the plastic wrap closed. Repeat with the rest of the cheese to make another log. Refrigerate the logs for at least 3 hours and up to 3 days.

3. To prepare the mushrooms: In a large sauté pan, heat 1 tablespoon of the oil over high heat. Add a third of each of the mushrooms, season with salt and pepper, and cook for 6 to 8 minutes, or until the mushrooms develop a golden crust. At this point, lift the mushrooms from the pan and set aside. Add more oil and cook the next batch of mushrooms. Repeat with the rest of the mushrooms and oil.

4. Reduce the heat to medium and add the shallots to the pan. Return the mushrooms to the pan and cook for about 7 minutes or until the shallots are translucent.

5. Add the stock, vinegar, and thyme leaves, increase the heat to high, and simmer rapidly for 9 to 10 minutes, or until the liquid reduces to about ½ cup. The mushrooms should be juicy but without much extra sauce.

6. Remove the cheese logs from the refrigerator and slice into rounds about ¾ inch thick. (This is very easy to do with dental floss.) Reserve any extra for another use.

7. Put about 1 cup of the mushroom mixture into each of 4 microwave-safe serving bowls. Top each serving with 1 or 2 rounds of cheese. Microwave for about 1 minute, or until the cheese softens and the mushrooms are piping hot. Serve immediately.

Lobster Risotto

When we first opened, we pledged to make the best paella possible in a restaurant setting. This meant cooking the rice from scratch and using a very traditional pan, among other things. The result was a dish that had to be made for two or more and took half an hour. From day one, we were hit with requests for "paella for one" or were told, "We forgot to order the paella; could we get one now?"

Rather than fight it, Andy came up with Lobster Risotto, our version of paella-for-one made with parcooked Arborio rice, which can be made quickly in the restaurant and in any quantity. It has become a huge seller. It's not authentic and not inexpensive, but it provides "affordable luxury." It's a great-tasting lobster dish, made with the same care as a dish that takes much longer to make, and is perfect if you want to impress someone. If you prefer, substitute fish or chicken stock for the homemade lobster stock called for here.

Serves 4

Lobster

One 1½-pound live lobster

½ cup olive oil

¾ cup tomato paste

2 carrots, peeled and coarsely chopped

2 ribs celery, coarsely chopped

1 large Spanish onion, coarsely chopped

1 head garlic, halved horizontally

6 sprigs fresh thyme

½ cup brandy

About 3 quarts water

3 fresh or dry bay leaves

8 black peppercorns

Risotto

½ cup (1 stick) plus 3 tablespoons unsalted butter

2 Spanish onions, finely diced

Kosher salt

1½ cups Arborio rice

2 cups dry white wine

1½ cups chopped asparagus

3 cups sliced spinach leaves

½ cup diced tomato

1. To cook the lobster: In a large pot of boiling water set over high heat, submerge the lobster head first and cook for about 6 minutes, or until the shell begins to turn red. The lobster is not meant to be cooked completely at this point.

2. Lift the lobster from the boiling water and plunge it into a large bowl filled with ice and cold water for about 15 minutes to stop the cooking and cool the lobster. When cool, crack the lobster tail, body, and claws and pull the lobster meat from the shells. Cut the meat into chunks about ¾ inch thick and set aside.

3. Heat a large stockpot over medium-high heat. When hot, pour the olive oil into the pan and then sear all of the lobster shells for about 15 minutes, or until they darken in color and are very fragrant. Add the tomato paste and cook for about 6 minutes, stirring to coat the shells with tomato paste. With a heavy instrument, crush the lobster shells.

4. Add the carrots, celery, onion, garlic, and thyme and sauté for 8 to 10 minutes, or until the vegetables soften. Add the brandy and bring to a rapid simmer. With a wooden spoon, scrape the bottom of the pan to remove any browned bits and deglaze the pan. Add the water, bay

leaves, and peppercorns and bring to a boil over high heat. Reduce the heat and simmer gently for 3½ to 4 hours. At this point you will have 2 to 2½ quarts of liquid.

5. Strain the broth through a sieve into a large bowl or another pot. Discard the vegetables, peppercorns, bay leaves, and shells. Return the broth to a pot and keep hot over medium heat. If not using right away, cool the broth and refrigerate in a tightly lidded container for up to 2 days.

6. To make the risotto: In a large, deep sauté pan, melt ½ cup of the butter with the onions over medium heat. Turn the heat to low, season to taste with salt, and sauté the onions for about 8 minutes, or until tender.

7. Add the rice and sauté for about 5 minutes longer. Be sure the rice is well coated with the butter and onions. Add the wine, raise the heat to medium-high and, stirring constantly, cook for about 5 minutes, or until the wine evaporates.

8. Meanwhile, bring the lobster broth to a boil over medium-high heat. Adjust the heat to keep the broth simmering.

9. Add about ¾ cup of the broth to the rice and stir until the liquid is absorbed. Add another ¾ cup of broth to the rice and stir until it is absorbed. Continue this process for about 20 minutes, or until the rice is tender but still with some bite and you have used 1 to 1½ quarts of the broth.

10. In another sauté pan, reduce about 2 cups of the remaining broth to about ½ cup thick liquid. Add the remaining 3 tablespoons of cold butter in chunks, whisking the whole time, until the butter sauce is thick. Season with salt and pepper.

11. Add the lobster meat to the butter sauce and heat through on the lowest possible heat for about 2 minutes. Remove the pan from the heat.

12. Meanwhile, in a saucepan of boiling water, blanch the asparagus for 50 to 60 seconds, or until the color sets. Drain the asparagus. Stir the blanched asparagus, the spinach, and the tomato into the risotto and cook for about 3 minutes to give the ingredients time to heat.

13. To serve, spoon 1 to 1½ cups of risotto into each of 4 shallow bowls. Top each with a quarter of the lobster meat and some of the sauce. Or serve the risotto family style in a single serving dish.

Sherry-Braised Short Ribs with Autumn Vegetables

We think a single, perfectly cooked short rib (two if they are small) is just the right amount of meat. This recipe takes most of the day but is the kind of cooking that conjures up family and farmhouses, and you can make enough for several meals—short ribs refrigerate well and are delicious for the next few days. You will have enough brine to quadruple this recipe for a big party or to make it a few more times over the next week. This is also a great template for all braises: pot roast, coq au vin, and anything cooked long and slow.

Serves 6

Brine and Ribs

1 small rib celery, coarsely chopped

½ small carrot, peeled and coarsely chopped

½ small Spanish onion, coarsely chopped

½ small head garlic, halved

3 sprigs fresh flat-leaf parsley, coarsely chopped

2 sprigs fresh thyme, coarsely chopped

1 small sprig fresh rosemary, coarsely chopped

1 cups apple cider

¾ cup cream sherry or another sweet sherry

2 tablespoons sherry vinegar

4 black peppercorns

1 bay leaf

2 teaspoons kosher salt

Six 4-inch-long beef short ribs

Vegetables

1 pint (2 cups) pearl onions

2 Yukon Gold potatoes

2 parsnips, peeled and cut into ¾-inch dice

2 carrots, peeled and cut into ¾-inch dice

1 celery root, peeled and cut into ¾-inch dice

1 turnip, peeled and cut into ¾-inch dice

3 tablespoons olive oil

Kosher salt and freshly ground black pepper

Braising

2 cups instant flour or all-purpose flour

½ cup high-quality Spanish paprika (not smoked paprika)

¼ cup chili powder

3 teaspoons kosher salt

1½ teaspoons cayenne

¾ cup olive oil

5 cups veal stock

1. In a large nonreactive bowl or deep plastic container, toss the celery, carrot, onion, and garlic with the parsley, thyme, and rosemary.

2. Add the apple cider, sherry, vinegar, peppercorns, bay leaves, and salt, and stir well.

3. Lay the ribs, meat side down, in one or more large, shallow nonreactive dish(es) or pan(s). Pour the brine over the ribs, refrigerating any extra in a lidded container for up to a week for another use (or discard it). Cover the ribs with a lid or plastic wrap and refrigerate for at least 8 hours and up to 2 days.

4. To roast the vegetables: Preheat the oven to 450°F.

5. Make an X in the root end of each pearl onion. Drop the onions into a pot of well-salted boiling water and blanch over high heat for 3 to 4 minutes. Drain and slice the root end from the onions. The skin should follow. Set the onions aside.

6. In a mixing bowl, toss the potatoes, parsnips, carrots, celery root, and turnip with 2 tablespoons of the olive oil. Season to taste with salt and pepper and mix well.

7. Spread the remaining tablespoon of olive oil in a shallow baking pan and then spread the vegetables over the pan in a single layer. You may need to use 2 pans, depending on their size, and a little more olive oil. Roast the vegetables for about 10 minutes. Stir the vegetables, rotate the pans, and roast for 10 to 15 minutes longer, or until they are tender and golden brown.

8. Use immediately or let the vegetables cool in the pans. Transfer to a tightly lidded storage container and refrigerate for up to 2 days.

9. To braise the short ribs: preheat the oven to 375°F.

10. In a 1-gallon resealable plastic bag, combine the flour, paprika, chili powder, salt, and cayenne. Seal the bag and shake the mixture to blend.

11. Lift the ribs from the brine and pat dry with a clean kitchen towel. Reserve the brine.

12. Drop 2 ribs at a time into the bag, shake to coat well, and then remove.

13. Heat a roasting pan on 2 burners over medium-high heat. Add the olive oil and, when hot, brown the ribs until golden brown on all sides. You might have to do this in batches, depending on the size of the pan.

14. Pour the oil from the pan, wipe any cooked flour from the pan, and scrape the edges and bottom of the pan.

15. Return the short ribs to the pan and pour 1 cup of the reserved brine and the veal stock over them. Cover the pan with aluminum foil and bring to a boil. Very carefully, transfer the roasting pan to the oven and braise for about 1½ hours, or until the ribs are tender. Lift the ribs from the pan and set them aside. Set the pan aside to allow the braising liquid to cool.

16. Holding a fine-mesh sieve over a bowl, strain the braising liquid. Skim as much of the fat from the braising liquid with a spoon or ladle or put the liquid in the freezer for an hour and then lift off the fat that congeals on the surface.

17. Raise the oven temperature to 425°F.

18. Put the short ribs, onions, reserved roasted vegetables, and strained liquid in the roasting pan and bring to a boil on top of the stove. Return the pan to the oven and roast for 35 to 40 minutes, or until a knife inserted into the center of the ribs comes out hot.

19. On 6 serving plates or a large platter, arrange the short ribs. Serve each plate with about ¾ cup of the roasted vegetables and then with a ladleful of braising liquid.

Crab Cakes

The best crab cake is crabmeat held together with as few other ingredients as possible. This one is a variant of the one Alain Sailhac taught Andy to make at the 21 Club back in the 1980s. If you have a good fish store, ask for unpasteurized jumbo lump crabmeat and try not to break up the pieces when mixing the ingredients. Use a nonstick pan, turn them only once, and finish them in the oven to avoid handling them any more than necessary.

Serves 6

1 pound lump crabmeat

1 large egg, lightly beaten

¼ cup panko (Japanese bread crumbs)

¼ cup diced onion

¼ cup diced red bell pepper

3 tablespoons mayonnaise

1 tablespoon Dijon mustard

1 tablespoon chopped fresh flat-leaf parsley

1 teaspoon Old Bay seasoning

Kosher salt and freshly ground black pepper

¼ cup instant flour or cake flour

¼ cup semolina flour

3 tablespoons olive oil

3 cups mesclun greens (optional)

6 tablespoons Barcelona Aïoli (page 65)

1. Gently pick through the crabmeat to make sure there are no shells. As you do so, be careful to leave it in lumps, not flakes.

2. Transfer the crabmeat to a medium mixing bowl and add the egg, bread crumbs, onion, bell pepper, mayonnaise, mustard, parsley, and Old Bay seasoning. Using your fingers, mix well and take care not to break up the crabmeat. Season to taste with salt and pepper.

3. Form the crab mixture into 6 crab cakes. As you form them, use your forefinger and thumb to squeeze the sides of the cakes to raise them in the middle. Refrigerate the crab cakes for at least 1 hour and up to 24 hours.

4. Preheat the oven to 375°F.

5. In a shallow bowl, stir together the flour and semolina. Dust the chilled crab cakes with the flour mixture, coating both sides.

6. In a large, nonstick, ovenproof sauté pan, heat the olive oil over medium heat and cook the crab cakes for about 5 minutes, or until lightly browned. Turn and transfer to the oven for 5 to 6 minutes longer, or until browned on both sides.

7. Divide the mesclun greens among 6 serving plates. Put a crab cake on top of the greens and then spoon about a tablespoon of aïoli on each cake and serve.

Empanadas with Smoked Pepper Sauce

You can put anything inside an empanada: eggs, lobster, fish, oxtail . . . we've done it all. This is our staple empanada, from a recipe Andy came up with the day before we opened. The meat is spicy but not overly so. We deep-fry them, but they can also be baked in the oven—a bonus for the home chef. It is *vital* that the meat mixture be completely chilled before filling the empanada. It is the retention of the fat until the first bite that makes these so juicy and good.

Serves 8

Dough

6 cups all-purpose flour

3 tablespoons sugar

1 tablespoon kosher salt

1 teaspoon baking powder

2 large eggs

2 egg yolks

½ cup red wine vinegar

1 cup (2 sticks) unsalted
butter, melted and cooled

1¼ cups water

Meat Mixture

3 tablespoons olive oil

5 ribs celery, finely diced

3 cloves garlic, crushed and minced

2 carrots, peeled and finely diced

1 large Spanish onion, finely diced

Kosher salt and freshly
ground black pepper

3 pounds ground beef,
preferably with 20 percent fat

One 35-ounce can Italian
plum tomatoes

½ cup ketchup

1 tablespoon ancho chile powder

One 4-ounce can chipotle
chiles in adobo

Assembly

About 2 cups all-purpose
flour, for rolling

3 large eggs

2 tablespoons water

About 5 cups cornmeal, for baking

5 cups soybean or canola
oil, for deep frying

1½ cups warm Smoked Pepper
Sauce (recipe follows)

1. To make the dough: In the bowl of an electric mixer fitted with the dough hook or paddle attachment and set on low speed, mix the flour, sugar, salt, and baking powder until well incorporated.

2. In a small bowl, whisk together the eggs, egg yolks, and vinegar.

3. Add the egg mixture and the melted butter to the flour and mix for about 1 minute, until blended. Increase the speed to medium and add the water. Mix for about 2 minutes to incorporate fully.

4. Scrape the dough onto a lightly floured work surface and divide into 3 equal portions. Shape each into a rounded disk and wrap in plastic wrap. Refrigerate for at least 4 hours and up to 3 days.

5. To prepare the meat filling: In a large sauté pan, heat the olive oil over medium heat. Add the celery, garlic, carrots, and onion and season to taste with salt and pepper. Cook, stirring, for about 7 minutes, or until the vegetables are soft and the onion is translucent.

6. Crumble the meat into the pan, season with about ½ teaspoon of salt and some pepper, and cook over low heat, breaking up with a wooden spoon, for 10 to 12 minutes, or until the meat is cooked through with no pink showing.

7. Meanwhile, empty the tomatoes and their juice into a mixing bowl and, using your hands, crush the tomatoes. Add the tomatoes and the juice to the sauté pan. Add the ketchup and the chile powder and stir to mix.

8. Remove the chipotle chiles from the can and chop well. Add the chiles and the adobe sauce from the can to the meat and bring to a simmer. Taste and adjust the seasoning with salt and pepper.

9. Transfer the meat mixture to a shallow pan and set aside to cool. Refrigerate for at least 2 hours, until well chilled, and up to 3 days.

10. To assemble the empanadas: Let the dough sit at room temperature for 20 to 30 minutes.

11. Dust a work surface and rolling pin with flour and roll 1 piece of dough quite thin (about ⅛ inch thick). Lightly flour a 4-inch round cookie or biscuit cutter and cut out as many rounds as possible. Gather any scraps, reroll, and cut out more rounds. You should get 8 to 10 from each piece of dough.

12. Continue with the 2 remaining pieces of dough. You will have 24 to 30 rounds when you are done.

13. In a small bowl, whisk the eggs with the water.

14. Lay the dough circles on a lightly floured work surface. Brush the edges of each one with the egg wash. Spoon 2½ to 3 tablespoons of the chilled meat mixture into the center of each round of dough. Fold the dough over the filling to form a semicircle and press the edges together. With a fork that has been dipped in flour, crimp the edges of the empanadas.

15. Put the empanadas on baking sheets generously dusted with cornmeal and refrigerate them for at least 45 minutes, or until chilled.

16. Preheat the oven to 200°F.

17. In a deep, heavy pot, heat the oil over high heat until it registers 385°F on a deep-fat thermometer. When hot, fry 5 or 6 empanadas at a time for 4 to 5 minutes, or until browned and crisp. Lift the empanadas from the oil with a slotted spoon and drain on a paper towel–lined baking sheet. Let the oil return to 385°F between batches. Keep the fried empanadas warm in the oven while you fry the remaining batches.

18. Pile the empanadas on a platter. Pour the warm pepper sauce into a bowl and serve with the empanadas for dipping.

smoked pepper sauce

Makes about 5 cups

3 tablespoons olive oil

1 large Spanish onion, thinly sliced

3 cloves garlic, crushed

One 35-ounce can Italian plum tomatoes

Two 15-ounce jars or cans roasted red peppers,
drained and coarsely chopped

3 chipotle chiles in adobo

2 tablespoon adobo sauce from the can of chipotle chiles

Kosher salt and freshly ground black pepper

1. In a saucepan, heat the olive oil over medium heat. Add the onion and garlic and cook for 5 to 7 minutes, or until the onion is translucent and tender.

2. Meanwhile, empty the tomatoes and their juice into a mixing bowl and, using your hands, crush the tomatoes. Add the tomatoes and their juice, the roasted red peppers, chipotle chiles, and adobo sauce. Season to taste with salt and pepper. Lower the heat to medium-low and simmer the sauce for about 30 minutes, stirring constantly and tending carefully, until the sauce is slightly thickened and the flavors blend.

3. Remove the pan from the heat and let the sauce cool for about 20 minutes.

4. Working in batches, transfer the sauce to a blender and puree until smooth.

5. Return the sauce to the pan and reheat gently until warm, if necessary, or store the pureed sauce in an airtight container and refrigerate for up to 2 days. Reheat gently before using, just until warm.

Chicken Livers with Poblano Peppers and Balsamic Vinegar

It never ceases to amaze us how much people love chicken livers. Antonio Saldana, our chef in Norwalk, put this dish together using a Mexican recipe that he liked and the traditional chicken livers–and–balsamic vinegar that we had made for years. Be careful not to overcook the livers. By the time they are well seared on a home stove, they should be done. Take them out of the pan and set them aside while you finish the sauce.

Serves 4

1 pound chicken livers, patted dry

Kosher salt and freshly
ground black pepper

2 tablespoons olive oil

1 poblano pepper, seeded,
cored, and cut into thin strips

3 tablespoons sliced shallots
(about 2 shallots)

¼ cup balsamic vinegar

1. Season the livers with salt and pepper.

2. In a large sauté pan, heat the olive oil over high heat. Sear the livers for 3 to 4 minutes without turning. Add the pepper strips and shallots, turn the livers over, and sear for 2 minutes longer. Remove the livers from the pan.

3. Add the vinegar to the pan and, using a wooden spoon, scrape up any browned bits sticking to the bottom of the pan. Cook for 2 to 3 minutes, or until the vinegar reduces and thickens slightly. Return the livers to the pan and heat if necessary.

4. Spoon the livers and vegetables onto 4 serving plates. Drizzle the pan juices over and around the livers and serve.

Spinach and Chickpea Casserole

This is a longtime favorite, brought to us by a chef named José Palacios from Spain. It is more North African than European in taste, which makes it very authentically Andalusian. It's a favorite among vegetarians and is more an addition to a meal than a centerpiece. Try to use good, fresh cumin; it makes a big difference.

Serves 6

2 tablespoons plus
1½ teaspoons kosher salt

5 pounds baby spinach leaves

½ day-old round loaf Italian bread, crust removed and bread cut into cubes (about 6 cups)

1¾ cups extra-virgin olive oil

10 cloves garlic

1 tablespoon ground cumin

1 teaspoon freshly grated nutmeg

One 15-ounce can chickpeas, drained

1. Preheat the oven to 425°F.

2. Bring a large pot of water with 2 tablespoons of salt to a boil over high heat. Set a large bowl of ice water near the stove. Working in batches and using tongs, dunk the spinach leaves into the water for no longer than 1 minute to set the color. Lift them from the water and immediately plunge in the ice water to stop the cooking. Continue until all the spinach is blanched. Squeeze the water from the spinach and transfer to a food processor fitted with the metal blade.

3. Put the bread cubes in a medium bowl and pour ¾ cup of the olive oil over them. Toss to mix so that the bread absorbs the olive oil and then spread the bread cubes in a single layer on a jelly-roll or similar pan and bake for about 25 minutes, stirring often, until very crisp and golden brown. When done, let the bread cubes cool on the baking sheet.

4. Meanwhile, in a medium saucepan, heat the remaining cup of olive oil over medium-low heat. Cook the garlic cloves for 7 to 10 minutes, or until golden brown and tender. Watch carefully to prevent burning. Transfer the garlic and the oil to the food processor. Add the bread cubes, cumin, nutmeg, and remaining 1½ teaspoons of salt to the bowl and process for 3 to 5 minutes, or until smooth and paste-like. Taste and adjust the seasonings.

5. Spoon the spinach mixture into a serving bowl. Stir the drained chickpeas into the pureed mixture, cover, and refrigerate for at least 2 hours, or until chilled, and up to 2 days.

6. When ready to serve, spoon the spinach and chickpea mixture into 6 microwave-safe serving bowls or 1 large serving bowl. Microwave on high power for 3 to 4 minutes, or until piping hot. Serve immediately.

Costillas de Cerdo

Chef Lisa Varnberg developed this recipe and the all-purpose barbecue glaze. The ribs can be baby back ribs or the larger St. Louis spareribs that we prefer. We like to have families eat at Barcelona, and these ribs are great to have on the menu for the preteen crowd.

Serves 4

Spice Mix

1 tablespoon ground anise

1 tablespoon dry mustard

1 tablespoon sugar

2 teaspoons sweet smoked paprika (*pimentón de la vera dulce*)

1 teaspoon kosher salt

Spareribs

1 rack pork spareribs (12 to 13 ribs)

Juice of 4 oranges

Juice of 2 lemons

¾ cup honey

½ cup sherry vinegar

⅛ cup oloroso (sweet) sherry

2 tablespoons hot smoked paprika (*pimentón de la vera picante*)

3 teaspoons ground anise

½ cup water

1. To make the spice mix: In a small mixing bowl, stir together the anise, mustard, sugar, paprika, and salt.

2. Rub the ribs on all sides with the spice mixture. Set aside in a nonreactive dish to marinate for 1 hour or refrigerate for up to 24 hours.

3. Preheat the oven to 300°F.

4. Put the ribs in a shallow baking dish and roast for 2 hours, or until the meat easily pulls away from the bones.

5. Meanwhile, in a nonreactive saucepan, combine the orange juice, lemon juice, honey, vinegar, sherry, paprika, and anise and bring to a simmer over medium heat. Simmer for about 25 minutes, stirring frequently. Cover to keep warm and set aside.

6. Raise the oven temperature to 425°F.

7. Lay the ribs in a large, deep, ovenproof sauté pan and pour the sauce over the ribs. Add the water and roast the ribs for about 15 minutes, or until the ribs are heated through and the sauce reduces to a glaze.

8. Watch that the ribs do not scorch and, if the sauce reduces too much, add a little more water.

9. Stack 4 ribs in the center of each plate and spoon the pan sauce over them.

Cauliflower and Fennel Cazuela

This dish was developed by Tim Hallama, who was our opening chef in West Hartford. Although it's an Italian-inspired vegetable dish, it fits perfectly on our menu because there are a surprising number of cauliflower fans out there. When it gets cold outside, this becomes a top seller. You can make everything ahead and then heat and serve. Cazuelas are earthenware dishes traditionally used in Spain for casseroles, soups, and similar dishes. The word also refers to a South American and Spanish soup or stew.

Serves 4 to 6

1 head cauliflower, divided into bite-sized florets (about 4½ cups)

1 bulb fennel, fronds removed and bulbs halved

6 tablespoons olive oil

Kosher salt and freshly ground pepper

1 small Spanish onion, thinly sliced

4 cloves garlic, chopped

1½ cups heavy cream

¾ cup panko (Japanese bread crumbs)

2 teaspoons freshly squeezed lemon juice

¾ cup grated Manchego or Parmesan cheese

2 teaspoons chopped fresh flat-leaf parsley

1 teaspoon chopped fresh thyme leave

Bread Crumb Topping

½ cup olive oil

10 cloves garlic, thinly sliced

3 cups panko (Japanese bread crumbs)

Pinch of hot red pepper flakes

Kosher salt and freshly ground black pepper

¾ cup grated Parmesan cheese

2 tablespoons chopped fresh flat-leaf parsley

2 teaspoons chopped fresh thyme

2 tablespoons chopped fresh chives, for garnish

1 tablespoon extra-virgin olive oil, for garnish

1. Prepare a charcoal or gas grill so that the charcoal or heating element is medium hot. Lightly spray the grilling rack with vegetable oil spray to prevent sticking. As an alternative, preheat the broiler.

2. In a pot of lightly salted boiling water, blanch the cauliflower for about 7 minutes. Remove with a slotted spoon and plunge into a bowl of ice water. Drain and set aside.

3. In the same pot with the water boiling, blanch the fennel for about 5 minutes. Remove with a slotted spoon and plunge into a bowl of ice water. Drain.

4. Lightly rub about 1 tablespoon of the olive oil on each fennel half and season lightly with salt and pepper. Grill, cut side down, for 5 to 7 minutes, or until there are good grill marks. Cut each bulb into very thin strips, ⅛ to ¼ inch thick, and set aside.

5. In a large skillet, heat the remaining ¼ cup of olive oil over medium-low heat. Add the onion slices to the pan, season with salt, and cook for about 10 minutes, until softened.

6. Add the garlic and cook slowly for 8 to 10 minutes longer, or until the garlic is softened but not colored and the onions are very soft.

7. Add the blanched cauliflower florets and julienned fennel, season well with salt and pepper, and cook slowly for 15 to 20 minutes longer, or until the vegetables are tender and can be crushed with the back of a spoon.

8. Add the cream, bread crumbs, and lemon juice. Season to taste with salt and pepper and stir in the cheese, parsley, and thyme. When heated through and the cheese is melted, remove from the heat and set aside.

9. Preheat the oven to 400°F.

10. To make the bread crumb topping: In a large sauté pan, heat the olive oil over medium-low heat. When hot, add the garlic and cook for 5 to 7 minutes, or until the garlic is honey colored.

11. Add the bread crumbs and pepper flakes and season to taste with salt and pepper. Cook for 7 to 10 minutes longer, or until the bread crumbs are honey brown. Watch carefully and stir frequently to prevent sticking and burning.

12. Add the cheese, parsley, and thyme; mix well and remove from the heat.

13. Fill four to six 6-ounce ramekins or a single casserole dish with the cauliflower mixture, leaving a ¼-inch rim. Top each with about ¼ cup of the bread crumb topping. You may not use all the topping; store it in an airtight container for up to 2 weeks and use it to top casseroles or to bread poultry or pork. The dish can be made a day ahead up to this point.

14. Set the dishes on a baking sheet and bake for 15 to 20 minutes (or microwave on high power for about 3 minutes).

15. Serve garnished with chopped chives and a drizzle of extra-virgin olive oil.

SPANISH CHEESES

At their simplest, tapas are presented as plates of cheese and cured meats. Spaniards take immense pride in the variety of cheeses they produce, as well as in the artistry it takes to make them. Although Spanish artisanal craftsmen and craftswomen may not be as well known as those in neighboring France and Italy, they are every bit as skilled and dedicated.

Spanish cheeses are fashioned from cow's, sheep's, and goat's milk and aged in different environments that result in myriad flavors, colors, and textures. A small percentage of the country's finest cheeses are imported into the United States.

Many are available in supermarkets, while others are sold in specialty shops. If you live in a metropolitan area with a large Spanish population, you might be able to locate more of these cheeses than if you live in a small town. Many are available on the Internet as well.

spanish cheeses available in the united states

CABRALES: This is probably the best-known Spanish blue, with a pungent flavor and an appealing creaminess. It is cave-ripened, and as it ripens it becomes heavily blue veined.

GARROTXA: Americans are not as used to semifirm goat's milk cheeses as are Europeans, and Garrotxa is a good one to start with. It has a washed rind and rich mouthfeel and is only mildly acidic.

IBERICO: This three-milk cheese (cow, goat, and sheep) is covered with a characteristic black, stamped rind. The semifirm cheese is mild and pleasing.

IDIAZABAL: Produced in the Basque region, this lightly smoked sheep's milk cheese is hard and fairly sharp. It combines the flavors of sheep milk, nuts, and just a hint of smokiness.

LA LEYENDA: This creamy sheep's milk cheese is similar in flavor, texture, and appearance to French Brie. Like Brie, it becomes runny and delicious as it reaches room temperature.

LA SERENA: This soft, creamy, full-flavored sheep's milk cheese pairs well with bold Spanish red wines.

LEONORA: A fresh, mild, and soft goat's milk cheese, this is made in Leon.

MAHÓN: Aged Mahón cheese has a washed, molded rind and is a mild, semifirm cow's milk cheese produced on the Balearic Islands. In the United States, Mahón is more commonly available as a milder, fresher cheese.

MANCHEGO: Perhaps the most famous Spanish cheese, the sheep's milk cheese originally was produced in La Mancha, where the animals roam the endless, arid fields of Don Quixote. Manchego is now available in many varieties, including aged, rosemary covered, and brandy rubbed. It is a dependable, semifirm cheese with a subtle nutty flavor.

MONTENEBRO: This soft goat's milk cheese is coated with ash and allowed to develop a deep yet subtle flavor and a luscious creaminess. It is sold as a flattened log.

MURCIA AL VINO: This mild goat's milk cheese is wine cured and has a flavor that is reminiscent of Muenster cheese.

NEVAT: This goat's milk cheese is creamy and chalky and has a bloomed rind.

PITU: From Asturias, this soft sheep's milk cheese is pleasingly piquant and is available plain or flavored with paprika.

SAN SIMON: This conical cow's milk cheese is mildly smoked, and its creamy texture conveys the fresh flavor of the pasture.

TETILLA: This semisoft cow's milk cheese is fashioned in a traditional conical form. It is mild and creamy and pairs well with the spices in any number of cured meats.

URGELIA: Produced in the Catalan region from cow's milk, Urgelia is semisoft with a rather pungent flavor and aroma. The cheese pairs well with dry red or white Spanish wines, especially the effervescent Txacolina.

VALDEÓN: This lesser-known Spanish blue cheese characteristically is wrapped in chestnut leaves while it ages, which results in a nutty flavor and creamy texture. It is unmistakably reminiscent of Roquefort without the briny aftertaste.

Almejas con Chorizo

Clams are very Spanish, and in the United States we have only a small fraction of the choices they have in Iberia. Use littlenecks or Manila clams—not mahogany clams or cockles. Try to remove the clams from the pan as they open, so the first ones don't overcook. Don't despair if this takes longer than expected. The fresher the clams, the less quickly they will open.

Serves 4

24 littleneck or Manila clams

Two 4-inch-long links smoked Spanish chorizo sausage

2 tablespoons olive oil

3 cloves garlic, very thinly sliced (preferably with a mandoline)

2 cups dry white wine

Leaves from 5 sprigs fresh thyme, coarsely chopped

1. Scrub the clams under cold running water. Drain and dry the clams.

2. Slice the sausage links lengthwise into 3 pieces and then slice across the sausage pieces into strips about ½ inch wide.

3. Heat a large sauté pan over medium-high heat and, when hot, add the olive oil. Add the chorizo slices and sear for about 3 minutes, or until nicely browned. Add the garlic and cook for about 2 minutes, or until browned.

4. Add the clams, wine, and thyme, shake the pan carefully, and cover with a lid, aluminum foil, or a plate and cook for 7 to 8 minutes, or until all the clams have opened. (Discard any that do not open.) Using tongs or a slotted spoon, remove the clams from the pan and divide evenly among 4 shallow serving bowls or put in one large bowl.

5. Turn the heat to high and cook the sauce for 4 to 5 minutes, or until slightly reduced and thickened. Pour the sauce and sausage slices over the clams and serve.

Albondigas

Little kids with their parents at Barcelona are always delighted to discover that one of Spain's classic dishes is meatballs in tomato sauce, called *albondigas*. We don't think there's a culture in the world that doesn't like good meatballs. The secret is to be generous with the fat (no substituting ground sirloin for the ground chuck and pork) and not overmix or overhandle the meatballs before cooking. Work them quickly and make sure they stay cold during the mixing process.

Serves 4

Tomato Sauce

1½ cups dry red wine

1½ cups veal or chicken stock

2 ounces Serrano ham, diced

3 anchovies

2 ribs celery, diced

1 carrot, peeled and diced

½ large Spanish onion, diced

¼ cup olive oil

5 cloves garlic, finely chopped

Two 35-ounce cans Italian plum tomatoes

1 bay leaf

Kosher salt and freshly ground black pepper

Meatballs

1 pound ground beef chuck

1 pound ground pork

2 cups panko (Japanese bread crumbs)

2 large eggs, lightly beaten

8 sprigs fresh flat-leaf parsley, tough stems discarded, finely minced

3 cloves garlic, finely minced

1 tablespoon dried oregano

¼ teaspoon kosher salt

Freshly ground black pepper

1. To make the sauce: In a small saucepan, bring the wine and stock to a boil over high heat. Cook at a rapid boil for about 7 minutes, or until reduced by half. Set aside.

2. In a food processor fitted with the metal blade, puree the ham, anchovies, celery, carrot, and onion until almost the consistency of paste.

3. In a deep saucepan, heat the olive oil over medium-low heat. Add the chopped garlic and cook for 3 to 4 minutes, stirring constantly, or until the garlic is golden brown.

4. Scrape the pureed vegetables and ham into the deep saucepan and cook, stirring, for 6 to 8 minutes, or until the vegetables are nicely browned and caramelized.

5. Pour the reduced wine and stock into the pan and bring to a simmer over medium-high heat, scraping the bottom of the pan with a wooden spoon to release any browned bits.

6. Meanwhile, empty the tomatoes and their juice into a mixing bowl and, using your hands, crush the tomatoes. Add the tomatoes and bay leaf to the sauté pan, reduce the heat to medium-low, and simmer gently for 30 to 40 minutes, or until slightly thickened and the flavors blend. Adjust the heat up or down to maintain the simmer. Season to taste with salt and pepper.

7. Set aside until needed or cool and transfer to a lidded container and refrigerate for up to 3 days.

8. To make the meatballs: Preheat the oven to 350°F.

9. In a large mixing bowl and using your hands or a wooden spoon, mix together the ground beef and pork, bread crumbs, eggs, parsley, garlic, and oregano. Season with the salt and pepper. To taste for seasoning, cook a small amount in a pan.

10. Roll the meat into meatballs about 1 inch in diameter and put them in a single layer in a shallow baking pan. Bake for 25 to 30 minutes, at which time the meatballs will be only partially cooked through.

11. Put the meatballs in the tomato sauce and simmer over medium-low heat, stirring constantly and taking care not to break up the meatballs, for about 20 minutes, or until the meatballs are cooked through. (If the sauce was refrigerated, reheat it slowly before adding the meatballs. It should be warm.)

12. Spoon 5 or 6 meatballs and sauce into 4 bowls and serve.

Warm Octopus Salad with Fingerling Potatoes and Smoked Paprika

This is authentic *pulpo gallego*—the way octopus is served in bars and country restaurants, dressed only with good paprika and salt. We have added potatoes to the dish, but you can omit them and just eat the octopus chunks with toothpicks, as they do in tapas bars in San Sebastian. Use *only* real *pimentón de la vera picante* and *pimentón de la vera dulce* and try to find good Portuguese octopus and not the Indonesian or Philippine substitute. It stays much more tender through the second cooking. Search for *pimentón* online or in Spanish markets and for octopus in good supermarkets and fish stores.

Serves 6 to 8

Octopus

One 4- to 6-pound Portuguese or Spanish octopus

3 ribs celery, coarsely chopped

1 Spanish onion, coarsely chopped

1 carrot, peeled and coarsely chopped

1 head garlic

2 cups dry white wine

¼ cup salt

3 bay leaves

8 black peppercorns

Octopus Salad

1 pound fingerling potatoes

3 tablespoons kosher salt

2 tablespoons extra-virgin olive oil

1 teaspoon hot smoked paprika (*pimentón de la vera picante*)

1 teaspoon sweet smoked paprika (*pimentón de la vera dulce*)

Juice of 1 lemon

1 red onion, thinly sliced

¼ bunch fresh marjoram, leaves chopped

Sea salt, for garnish

1. To cook the octopus: In a large, heavy pot, combine the octopus with the celery, onion, and carrot. Cut the garlic head in half horizontally and add to the pot.

2. Add the salt, wine, bay leaves, and peppercorns and then add enough cold water to cover the octopus by about 3 inches. Weight the octopus with a heavy plate.

3. Bring the liquid to a robust simmer over medium-high heat and cook for about 1½ hours, or until the octopus is tender. Adjust the heat up or down to maintain the simmer.

4. Lift the octopus from the pot and set aside to cool. When almost cool, cover and refrigerate until chilled or for up to 2 days.

5. To prepare the salad: Put the potatoes in a pot and add enough cold water to cover by 1 or 2 inches. Add the salt and bring the water to a boil over high heat. Reduce the heat and simmer for about 20 minutes, or until fork tender. Drain and let the potatoes cool. When cool enough to handle, slice in half horizontally.

6. Separate the legs from the body of the chilled octopus and cut each leg into 2½-inch-long sections. Cut each section in half horizontally. Discard the body.

7. Heat a large sauté pan over medium-low heat and, when hot, put 6 to 8 pieces of octopus in the pan with 6 pieces of potato. Add the olive oil and slowly and carefully swirl the pan for 2 or 3 minutes. Do not let either the octopus or the potatoes take on any color.

8. Add the paprikas and lemon juice to the pan and swirl the pan for about 1 minute to distribute them. Season the octopus well.

9. Remove the pan from the heat and toss in the onion and marjoram.

10. Divide the warm salad among 6 to 8 serving plates and garnish each serving with a pinch of sea salt.

Catalan Potatoes Bravas

Fried potato chunks dipped in mayonnaise are as traditional as Spanish food gets. The addition of the spicy red sauce makes these *bravas*, or "fierce." You can play with the colored sauces to vary the presentation. We bake the potatoes in this recipe, but if you prefer authenticity, you can deep-fry them (see Note).

Serves 4

1½ pounds waxy potatoes, such as Yukon Gold, red-skin, or fingerling potatoes

Kosher salt

¼ cup extra-virgin olive oil

2 large Spanish onions, thinly sliced

6 cloves garlic, chopped

2 teaspoons sweet smoked paprika (*pimentón de la vera dulce*)

1 teaspoon hot smoked paprika (*pimentón de la vera picante*)

1 teaspoon ground cumin

¼ teaspoon cayenne

Freshly ground black pepper

One 35-ounce can plum tomatoes

1 ½ tablespoons sherry vinegar

1 cup olive oil

Sea salt, for garnish

Barcelona Aïoli (page 65), for serving

1. Preheat the oven to 450°F.

2. Put the potatoes in a large pot and add enough cold water to cover by an inch. Add 4 tablespoons of salt and bring to a boil over high heat. Reduce the heat slightly and simmer for about 20 minutes, or until just fork tender. Drain the potatoes and set aside to cool. When cool, cut the potatoes into wedges or, if using fingerling potatoes, cut them in half lengthwise.

3. Meanwhile, in a large saucepan, heat the extra-virgin olive oil over medium heat. Add the onions and cook for about 10 minutes, or until they soften but have not colored. Add the garlic and cook gently for 6 to 8 minutes, or until the garlic is tender and aromatic. Stir in both paprikas, the cumin, and the cayenne. Season to taste with pepper.

4. Put the tomatoes and their juice in a bowl and, using your hands, crush the tomatoes slightly. Add the tomatoes, their juice, and the vinegar to the saucepan and season to taste with salt and pepper. Bring to a simmer over medium heat and cook for about 20 minutes, or until the sauce is heated through.

5. Let the tomato sauce cool a little and then, working in batches, puree it in a blender until smooth. As one batch is pureed, transfer it to a bowl or a container with a tight-fitting lid. Use the tomato sauce right away or refrigerate for up to 3 days.

6. In a large bowl, toss the cooled potatoes with the 1 cup of olive oil and season to taste with salt and pepper. Spread the potatoes and the oil in a shallow baking pan and roast for 12 to 15 minutes, or until the potatoes are nicely browned on one side. Rotate the pan and turn the potatoes over. Roast for 8 to 10 minutes longer, or until browned and crisp on the other side.

7. Spoon a liberal amount of cooled tomato sauce in the center of each of 4 serving plates. Mound the potatoes on top of the sauce and garnish with sea salt. Serve with the aïoli on the side.

Note: If you prefer fried potatoes, heat about 10 cups of canola or another vegetable oil in a deep, heavy pot until it registers 375°F on a deep-fat thermometer. If you don't have a thermometer, drop a small piece of potato into the oil, and if it bubbles around the edges of the potato, it's hot enough.

Meanwhile, preheat the oven to 250°F and line a baking sheet with several layers of paper towels.

Fry the potatoes in batches so that you don't crowd the pan. Carefully submerge them in the hot oil and let them cook for 4 to 6 minutes, or until crispy and browned. Lift the potatoes from the oil with a slotted spoon and let them drain on the paper towels. Sprinkle with salt and pepper and keep warm in the oven while you fry the remaining potatoes.

Morcilla Sausage with Caramelized Onions

We love morcilla—blood sausage—and when we put it on the menu we hope nobody asks what it is until they have eaten it. With a single bite, any doubts about it disappear, because it's truly delicious. We buy our blood sausage from an artisan sausage maker in New Haven, Connecticut, who makes it expressly for us. It usually can be found in ethnic neighborhoods with Polish, Italian, or German butchers. Barring that, it can also be found as "blood pudding" under several Irish brands.

Serves 4

3 large Spanish onions, thinly sliced

½ cup plus 3 tablespoons olive oil

¼ teaspoon kosher salt

2 cups balsamic vinegar

Twelve ½-inch-thick slices baguette

6 links sweet morcilla or other blood sausage

1. Preheat the oven to 400°F.

2. In a large ovenproof sauté pan, heat the onions, 3 tablespoons of the olive oil, and the salt over medium-low heat. Cook slowly for 7 to 10 minutes, stirring frequently, until the onions are translucent.

3. Put the pan in the oven and cook for about 25 minutes, stirring frequently, until the onions are golden brown. If they stick or some are getting too brown, add 2 tablespoons of water and scrape the onions from the pan's bottom. Remove from the oven and set aside until needed.

4. In a medium saucepan, cook the vinegar for 7 to 10 minutes over high heat, until it reduces by about two-thirds or boils with very large bubbles. Watch the vinegar carefully. Set aside.

5. Drizzle the remaining ½ cup of olive oil on both sides of the baguette slices and lay the slices on a baking sheet. Toast for 5 to 6 minutes, or until lightly browned. Rotate the baking sheet and turn the bread slices over. Toast for about 5 minutes longer, or until crispy and honey brown.

6. Slice each sausage link on the bias into 6 pieces, for a total of 36 slices.

7. In a large sauté pan over medium heat, lightly brown the sausage slices for 3 to 4 minutes on each side. Transfer to a plate; there is no need to drain the sausage.

8. Top each piece of toasted baguette with about 1½ tablespoons of onions and then with 3 overlapping slices of sausage. Arrange the tapas on a serving platter or individual serving plates, drizzle each with the reduced balsamic vinegar, and serve.

CURED MEATS

Cured meats are as commonplace at tapas bars across Spain as cheeses, olives, and seafood. For generations, Spanish home cooks, farmers, and restaurateurs have developed methods for curing meat that rival those of other European countries.

The most famous of Spain's cured meats is Serrano ham, and while there are far more complex jamóns, the first taste of Serrano is enough to sell most people on Spain's charcuterie. The subtle play of salt, pork essence and the sweet succulence of fat is irresistible.

spanish cured meats available in the united states

BUTIFARRA: This raw white sausage is so popular in Catalonia, where it is made, that you will find it at nearly every restaurant, where it will be grilled or boiled. Its flavor is similar to that of bratwurst, and it's just as versatile. At the Barca futbol game, it is served on a crusty baguette with mustard.

CANTIMPALO: This large, mild slicing chorizo is served similarly to salami.

CHISTORRA: Although this spicy little chorizo is referred to as a breakfast sausage, it's eaten all day long in Spain. It's made from lightly smoked pork and flavored with sweet smoked paprika.

DRIED CHORIZO: This popular sausage is available as a sweet or hot sausage, and both are used for cooking and slicing. Palacios is a brand commonly available in the United States. Chorizo is also the word used to mean "sausage."

FUET: The cured chorizo from Catalonia is studded with cracked pepper and served as a slicing sausage to eat with cheese, on bread, or as is.

IBERICO LOMO: The cured ham is served in sausage form. It's cut from the pork loin and then marinated and air dried once it's inside a sausage casing. It's great with firm cheeses and good bread.

JAMON IBERICO: Not too long ago, you could not buy this cured ham in the United States, but now it is imported. The best and most authentic is made from Black Iberian pigs that are allowed to roam through oak forests, where they eat mostly acorns, which contribute to the ham's rich, nutty flavor. Iberico is very expensive, but a little goes a long way; it's worth the extravagance now and again. Serve it with cheese and wine.

SALCHICHÓN DE VIC: This much revered hard sausage, similar to Italian salami, is made from lean pork and pepper as well as other seasonings. The best Salchichon comes from Vic, in the foothills of the Pyrenees. It's a slicing sausage with molded rind and sometimes sold stuffed with black truffles.

SERRANO HAM: Spain's favorite cured ham is air dried and is sold with or without the bone. While they cure, the hams are hung at room temperature with small cups suspended from their ends to catch the fat as it drips out of them. Serrano ham should be hand sliced as thin as possible and can be served as is or sautéed with vegetables.

SOBRASSADA: Manufactured on the Balearic Islands, this is a soft, raw, cured pork sausage richly spiced with paprika. Serve it as you would any robust salami.

the barcelona cookbook

Crispy Fried Whitebait

In Spain, tiny fresh fish with the heads on, fried and eaten whole, are a great communal snack. In this country they have always been a hard sell, which is a pity. Once you get past the "head on" part, they are addictive.

Serves 4

2 pounds fresh whitebait, rinsed and patted dry

2 to 3 cups milk

6 cups olive oil

3 cups instant flour (such as Wondra)

3 cups semolina flour

6 tablespoons kosher salt

1 tablespoon freshly ground black pepper

1 lemon, quartered, for serving

1. In a bowl large enough to hold the whitebait comfortably, cover the fish with milk. Use only enough to cover them barely and soak for at least 1 hour in the refrigerator.

2. In a deep, heavy pot, heat the oil over medium-low heat until a deep-fat thermometer registers 385°F. If you do not have a deep-fat thermometer, drop a single fish or a bread cube into the oil when it shimmers with heat. If the oil bubbles and dances around the food, it's ready.

3. While the oil is heating, mix the flours together in a large bowl and add the salt and pepper. Drain the whitebait and toss them in the flour mixture. When coated, transfer the fish to a colander or sieve and shake off the excess flour.

4. Working in batches, fry the fish for 3 to 4 minutes, or until lightly browned and crispy. Remove with a slotted spoon or the sieve and transfer to a paper towel to drain.

5. Serve the whitebait hot with lemon wedges.

Wild Salmon Paillard with Sweet-and-Sour Shallots

We like wild salmon, and this is a very simple way to highlight it. Wild salmon is seasonal, depending on when Alaska allows fishermen to catch them. It dries out faster than farmed salmon when cooked and so should be slightly rare in the middle when you take it out of the pan. These salmon paillards are so thin that they will finish cooking through on the plate. The sweet-and-sour shallots are really an escabeche, dressed up with French and Japanese ingredients.

Serves 6

Sweet-and-Sour Shallots

15 shallots, very thinly sliced (preferably with a mandoline)

1½ cups mirin (sweet Japanese rice cooking wine)

¼ cup pink peppercorns

¼ cup olive oil

3 tablespoons red wine vinegar

Salmon Paillards

18 ounces skinless wild king or coho salmon fillet

Kosher salt

1 teaspoon olive oil

Fresh chervil sprigs, for garnish

1. To make the sweet-and-sour shallots: In a medium saucepan, cover the shallots with the mirin and bring to a boil over medium-high heat. As soon as the mirin boils and the shallots wilt but do not cook all the way through, remove the pan from the heat.

2. With the back of a spoon, crush the peppercorns and add them to the pan with the olive oil and vinegar. Stir well and let the shallots cool. Transfer to a lidded container and refrigerate for about 2 hours, or until chilled. The shallots will keep for up to 4 days. Let the shallots reach room temperature before serving.

3. To make the paillards: Remove any pinbones from the salmon, using needle nose pliers. With a sharp slicing knife held at a 45-degree angle, slice the fillet on the bias into 6 pieces, each no more than ½ inch thick. Season both sides of each slice with a pinch of salt.

4. In a large nonstick sauté pan, heat the olive oil over high heat. When hot, add the salmon slices. Sear the salmon for 1 to 2 minutes on each side, or until cooked to the desired degree of doneness (but still slightly rare in the center).

5. Put the salmon paillards on 6 serving plates and spoon the shallots and juice over each one. Garnish with chervil sprigs and serve.

Piquillo Peppers Stuffed with Bacalao and Yukon Gold Potatoes

Piquillo peppers are small, sweet peppers grown in Navarra and prized throughout Spain for their assertive taste and texture. The very best are roasted over wood fires, peeled by hand, and sold in small jars or cans. They are a completely different product from the mass-produced piquillos packed in giant, #10 cans.

Similarly, the best bacalao is worlds apart from inexpensive, salty salt cod. In this dish, use the better products—it makes a difference. It takes two days to prepare, so you will have to plan well ahead of time. The potato-cod mixture is a simple version of the Provençal *brandade*.

Serves 6

Bacalao and Potatoes

¼ pound salt cod (bacalao)

1 rib celery, chopped

4 cloves garlic

5 or 6 black peppercorns

2 bay leaves

1 pound Yukon Gold potatoes

Kosher salt and freshly ground black pepper

¼ cup diced red onion

2 tablespoons chopped fresh flat-leaf parsley

1 tablespoon extra virgin olive oil

One 350-gram can piquillo peppers (about 12 ounces)

Saffron Aïoli

⅛ teaspoon saffron threads

¼ cup dry white wine

1½ cups mayonnaise

2 teaspoons freshly squeezed lemon juice

2 teaspoons chopped garlic

Kosher salt and freshly ground black pepper

1. To prepare the bacalao and potatoes: Put the salt cod in a pan and add water to cover. Refrigerate for 2 days, changing the water twice a day. The soaking softens, plumps, and removes most of the salt from the fish. When ready to prepare the dish, drain the fish.

2. In a large saucepan, mix together the celery, garlic, peppercorns, bay leaves and drained cod and add water to cover by about 1 inch. Bring to a gentle simmer over low heat and cook for 3 minutes. Adjust the heat to maintain a very gentle simmer.

3. Lift the fish from the saucepan, discard the cooking liquid, and let the fish cool. When cool enough to handle, use your fingers to flake the fish into large chunks.

4. Meanwhile, cook the potatoes in salted water to cover for 15 to 20 minutes, or until tender. (You can peel them first or not, as you prefer.) Drain, return the potatoes to the pan, and use a potato masher or fork to mash the potatoes coarsely. There should be some chunks left in the potatoes. Season to taste with salt and pepper.

5. Add the onion, parsley, and extra-virgin olive oil to the potatoes and mix well. Using a large spoon, spatula, or fork, gently fold the flaked fish into the potatoes, taking care not to break up the fish too much.

6. Drain the canned peppers and lay 12 of them flat on a cutting board.

7. Snip about 1 inch off the bottom corner of a sturdy plastic bag. Fill the bag with the potato mixture. Holding the bag like a pastry bag, squeeze the potato through the snipped corner into a pepper, filling it as full as you can. Continue until all 12 peppers are filled with potato. If you prefer, spoon the filling into the peppers.

8. For the saffron aïoli: In a small sauté pan, heat the saffron and wine over medium heat until the wine simmers. Simmer for 6 to 8 minutes, adjusting the heat to maintain the simmer. Remove from the heat and let the mixture cool slightly.

9. In a blender, puree the mayonnaise, lemon juice, garlic, and cooled wine and saffron mixture. Blend and season to taste with salt and pepper.

10. Put the peppers on a microwave-safe plate and microwave on high for about 3 minutes, or until hot. Put 2 peppers on each serving plate and serve with the saffron aïoli.

Calamari a la Plancha

We go through about 30,000 pounds of fresh calamari a year. Squid is seasonal—it's best in the summer through early fall—and there are times of the year it's very hard to find. We serve this dish only when we have fresh calamari, because the frozen product contains too much water and never really caramelizes the right way. Don't be shy with the seasonings; this is not supposed to be a subtle dish.

Serves 4

1 pound cleaned fresh calamari, cut into 1- to 1½-inch-thick rings, and tentacles, if included with the squid

Kosher salt

¼ cup olive oil

1½ tablespoons chopped garlic (3 to 5 cloves)

1 tablespoon chopped fresh flat-leaf parsley

⅛ teaspoon hot red pepper flakes

¼ cup extra-virgin olive oil

Sea salt, for garnish

4 lemon wedges, for garnish

1. Put 2 large sauté pans (cast iron if possible) over high heat for 3 to 4 minutes, or until very hot.

2. Pat the calamari dry with paper towels and then season lightly with salt.

3. Put 2 tablespoons of the olive oil in one of the pans and cook the calamari for about 4 minutes, or until it releases its liquid.

4. Put the remaining 2 tablespoons of olive oil in the other pan and then remove the pan from the heat and hold it, at an angle, near the pan with the calamari. Lift the calamari from the first pan with a slotted spoon and transfer to the second pan, leaving the juices in the first pan.

5. Return the second pan to the heat and add the garlic and tentacles. Cook until the calamari is nicely browned. Add the parsley and pepper flakes, stir, and remove the pan from the heat.

6. Divide the calamari among 4 serving plates, drizzle with extra-virgin olive oil, and garnish each plate with sea salt and a lemon wedge.

Calamari Stuffed with Saffron Rice, Chorizo, and Shrimp

Be careful not to stuff the squid too full, or the stuffing will pop out when the squid shrinks during cooking. For a truly impressive variation, stuff four squid tubes and four piquillo peppers and serve them side by side on a big white plate.

Serves 4

Squid

4 cups chicken stock

¼ teaspoon saffron threads

6 tablespoons olive oil

2 cups diced white onion
(2 to 3 onions)

Two 4-inch links smoked Spanish chorizo, diced into ¼-inch cubes

1½ cups short-grain rice, like Valencia or Arborio

Kosher salt and freshly ground black pepper

6 medium shrimp, peeled, deveined, and cut into ⅓-inch-long pieces

8 whole calamari, measuring 3 to 4 inches long, cleaned and skinned, tentacles reserved

Sauce

2 tablespoons olive oil

1 cup diced white onion

1 cup diced red bell pepper

Kosher salt and freshly ground black pepper

½ cup dry white wine

½ cup squid ink

1. To prepare the squid: In a medium saucepan, bring the chicken stock and saffron to a simmer over medium heat and cook for about 10 minutes. Adjust the heat to maintain the simmer.

2. In a deep sauté pan, heat 3 tablespoons of the olive oil over medium heat. Add the onion and chorizo and cook for about 7 minutes, or until the onions soften but do not color.

3. Add the rice and hot stock and cook for 3 to 4 minutes over medium-high heat, stirring frequently, until the stock comes to a boil. Season to taste with salt and pepper.

4. Reduce the heat to low, cover the pan with aluminum foil, and cook for about 20 minutes, or until the rice is tender and the stock is absorbed. Spread the rice over the bottom of a jelly-roll or similar pan and let it cool slightly.

5. In a small sauté pan, heat 1 tablespoon of the remaining olive oil over high heat. Add the shrimp, season with salt and pepper, and sear, stirring, just until the shrimp turns pink and opaque. Add to the rice and stir the shrimp and rice together. Let cool.

6. Put the squid tubes (bodies) on a work surface. Reserve the tentacles if you have them.

7. Snip about ¾ inch off the bottom corner of a sturdy plastic bag. Fill the bag with the rice mixture. Holding the bag like a pastry bag, squeeze the rice through the snipped corner into a squid tube, filling it as full as you can without overstuffing it. Secure the open end with a toothpick, weaving it through the flesh. Repeat until all tubes are filled. Cover with plastic wrap and refrigerate for up to 2 days.

8. To make the sauce: In another sauté pan, heat the olive oil over medium heat and cook the onion and bell pepper for about 7 minutes, or until the onion is translucent. Season to taste with salt and pepper.

9. Add the wine and squid ink to the pan and bring the liquid to a simmer over medium heat. Simmer for about 10 minutes and then transfer to a blender. Process until smooth and then return the sauce to the pan. Cover and keep warm. If the sauce becomes too thick as it sits, thin it with a tablespoon of water.

10. Preheat the oven to 400°F to finish preparing the squid.

11. Take the stuffed squid tubes from the refrigerator and season with salt and pepper.

12. In a large, ovenproof sauté pan, heat the remaining 2 tablespoons of olive oil over high heat and brown the squid on all sides. Add the tentacles to the pan and transfer the pan to the oven for about 8 minutes, or until the stuffing is heated through.

13. Spoon about ¼ cup of squid ink sauce down the center of each of 4 serving plates. Top the sauce with 2 squid tubes. Remove the toothpicks and serve with the tentacles.

Castilian Stew

This soup morphed from a classic *caldo gallego* over time, so that it looks like an authentic Spanish dish but is actually the invention of John Strong, one of our early chefs. Although John was Canadian, he understood the mind-set of the Spanish chef, with one foot anchored in tradition and the other in economy. His untimely death in 2005 left a void in the hearts of our employees and the soul of the company. Not a day goes by that we don't think of him. His stew is easy to make and includes lots of good, hearty ingredients. It's a winter lunch with a big piece of crusty bread.

Serves 4

½ pound ham, finely diced

½ pound slab bacon, finely diced

2 cups diced smoked Spanish chorizo sausage (about 4 links)

½ cup olive oil

¼ cup chopped garlic (see Note)

¼ cup chopped red bell pepper

2 cups canned tomatoes, drained

3 russet potatoes, peeled and diced (2½ to 3 cups)

5 to 6 cups chicken stock

Kosher salt and freshly ground black pepper

6 cups chopped escarole or a similar green (such as chard or kale) (about ½ pound)

1. In a large pot, cook the ham, bacon, chorizo, and olive oil over medium heat for 8 to 10 minutes. Add the garlic and red pepper and cook for 7 to 8 minutes longer.

2. With your hands, squeeze the tomatoes to break them up and expel their juices. Add them to the pot along with the potatoes and enough stock to cover. Bring to a simmer over medium heat and cook for about 15 minutes, or until the potatoes are tender. Season to taste with salt and pepper.

3. Push the greens into the soup and cook for about 10 minutes, until the greens wilt and the soup is piping hot. Taste for seasoning and serve.

Note: For ¼ cup of chopped garlic, use a whole head. Chop the peeled cloves in a food processor. To make the outer skins easy to remove, soak the cloves in water for about 6 hours. The skins will slide right off. Alternatively, heat them for about 20 seconds in a microwave and the garlic cloves will pop right out of the skins.

Roasted Garlic Bulbs with Bread

This is an original staple at Barcelona, and we still charge the same amount that we did back in 1996, when we opened our doors. When we make a new batch, the whole restaurant smells like roasting garlic, and few things smell better.

Serves 4

8 large heads garlic, excess outer papery skins discarded

4 sprigs fresh rosemary, coarsely chopped

6 sprigs fresh thyme, coarsely chopped

½ cup extra-virgin olive oil, plus more for drizzling

1½ teaspoons kosher salt

Sea salt and freshly ground black pepper

8 to 12 slices warm, crusty bread, for serving

1. Preheat the oven to 325°F.

2. Slice the top from each head of garlic to expose the cloves. Discard the tops. Put the garlic heads, exposed sides up, in a small baking dish.

3. Scatter the herbs over the garlic and then spoon about a tablespoon of olive oil over each head. Season with salt and pepper and cover the baking dish tightly with aluminum foil.

4. Roast the garlic for about 2 hours, or until the exposed cloves are tender and lightly browned.

5. Discard any excess skin still on the heads, but leave the garlic pulp encased in a thin membrane of skin. Put 2 heads on each of 4 plates and garnish with a drizzle of olive oil and a pinch of sea salt. Serve with the bread.

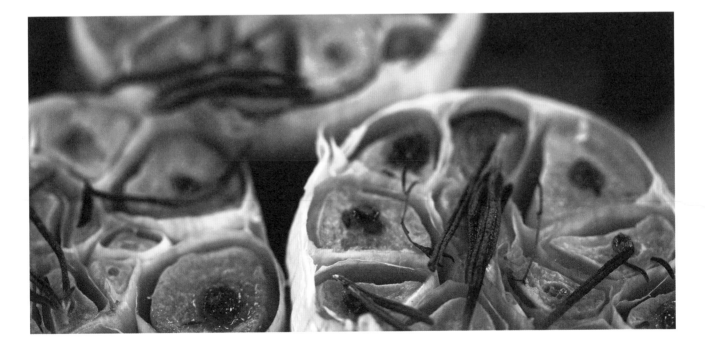

Tomato Fritters with Robiola Cheese and Shallot Vinaigrette

This dish will test your frying skills. A big, ripe tomato filled with runny cheese is not the simplest thing to fry, but the reward is in the eating. This makes a nice dinner during the summer. It's best to chill the tomatoes after assembly before frying.

Serves 4

Shallot Vinaigrette

6 shallots, peeled

¼ cup Dijon mustard

⅓ cup sherry vinegar

1½ cups olive oil

Kosher salt and freshly ground black pepper

Fritters

2 pounds large, ripe beefsteak tomatoes

¼ pound fresh robiola cheese

Kosher salt and freshly ground black pepper

3 cups all-purpose flour

5 large eggs, lightly beaten

3 cups panko (Japanese bread crumbs)

Vegetable oil, for deep frying

2 teaspoons sea salt, plus more for garnish

½ teaspoon sweet smoked paprika (*pimentón de la vera dulce*), for garnish

1. To make the shallot vinaigrette: Put the shallots, mustard, and vinegar into a blender and puree until smooth. With the motor running, slowly pour in the olive oil and blend until the vinaigrette is thickened and well mixed. Season to taste with salt and pepper. Set aside while you fry the fritters.

2. To make the tomato fritters: Core the tomatoes and cut each into ¼-inch-thick slices. Use only center cuts and keep all of similar sizes together. You need 8 slices for 4 fritters.

3. Rub half of the tomato slices with cheese and season each with salt and pepper. Top each cheese-topped slice with another slice of tomato, matching those of similar size. This will make 4 sandwiches of 2 slices each.

4. Spread the flour in a shallow bowl or plate, the eggs in another, and the bread crumbs in a third. Season the eggs with salt and pepper. Dip each tomato sandwich in the flour to coat on both sides and then in the eggs and the bread crumbs to coat all sides.

5. Pour vegetable oil into a large, heavy pot to a depth of approximately 3 inches. Heat over medium-high heat until a deep-fat thermometer registers 325°F. Very carefully and using a long-handled spatula, lower 1 or 2 fritters at a time into the hot oil and fry for 3 to 5 minutes on each side, or until golden brown. Use long-handled tongs to turn the fritters.

6. Remove the fritters from the oil with the spatula and drain on paper towels. Season with sea salt.

7. Put about 2 tablespoons of vinaigrette in the center of each of 4 plates and put a fritter on top of the sauce. Garnish with paprika and finish with sea salt.

Scallops with Brussels Sprouts

Brussels sprouts get a bad rap, but we put them on the menu every winter, and they fly out of the kitchen. When fresh and cooked right, they are sweet and flavorful. The best way to cook them is as leaves only, in butter and garlic. Be sure to buy "dry" sea scallops from a reputable fish store. The ones that have been soaked in a preservative will give off liquid and mess up the dish.

Serves 4

Kosher salt

½ pint (1 cup) Brussels sprouts, root end trimmed

12 giant dry scallops

Freshly ground black pepper

3 tablespoons unsalted butter

¼ pound slab bacon, rind removed and bacon cut into ½-inch dice

2 shallots, diced

1 teaspoon chopped garlic

¾ cup dry white wine

1. Bring a medium saucepan of water mixed with 2 teaspoons salt to a rapid boil over high heat. Put a bowl of ice water near the stove.

2. Cook the sprouts in the boiling water for about 3 minutes, just until bright green and still firm.

3. Drain the sprouts and plunge them into the ice water to stop the cooking. Drain and, when cool enough, separate the sprouts into leaves for cooking.

4. Remove the muscles from the scallops and then pat the scallops dry with a clean kitchen towel and season well with salt and pepper.

5. In a sauté pan set over high heat, heat 2 tablespoons of the butter until melted. Add the bacon to the pan and cook for about 2 minutes, turning once, or until the fat is rendered. Add the scallops to the pan in a single layer and sear for about 3 minutes, or until they develop a nice brown crust. After one side is browned, turn them.

6. Add the Brussels sprout leaves, shallots, and garlic to the pan and cook for 2 to 3 minutes, stirring, or until the scallops are opaque and cooked through. Season to taste with salt and pepper.

7. Add the wine to the pan and bring to a boil. Deglaze the pan by scraping the bottom with a wooden spoon to remove any browned bits.

8. With a slotted spoon, carefully lift the scallops from the pan and set aside.

9. Cook over high heat until the wine reduces by about two-thirds. Swirl the remaining tablespoon of butter in the pan and cook until melted.

10. Divide the scallops among 4 serving plates and pour the wine sauce and Brussels sprout leaves over them. Serve immediately.

Lamb Chops with Romesco Sauce

Lamb is a staple in Spain, to the point where there are restaurants that serve lamb and nothing else. For this tapa, we use the loin chop, which is the mini-T-bone, rather than the rack or rib chop, which is the lollipop-shaped one. At the restaurant we cut the chops thin for quick cooking, but for this recipe we recommend nice, medium-thick chops.

Serves 4

8 loin lamb chops, about ¾ inch thick

Kosher salt and freshly ground black pepper

4 cups baby arugula

Juice of ½ lemon

1½ tablespoons extra-virgin olive oil

3 cups Romesco Sauce, at room temperature (recipe follows)

1. Lightly spray the grates of your gas or charcoal grill with flavorless vegetable oil spray. Preheat the gas grill or prepare the charcoal grill so that the heating element or charcoal is hot. Alternatively, preheat the broiler.

2. Season the lamb chops on both sides with salt and pepper. Grill for 4 to 5 minutes, turn, and grill for an additional 3 minutes for medium-rare.

3. Meanwhile, in a large mixing bowl, toss the arugula with the lemon juice and extra-virgin olive oil. Season to taste with salt and pepper.

4. Spoon about ¾ cup of romesco sauce on the side of each of 4 serving plates. Put about 1 cup of arugula on the opposite side of the plate. Top the sauce with 2 lamb chops and serve immediately.

romesco sauce While we serve this robust, garlicky sauce with the lamb chops, we set it apart as a separate recipe because it's a marvelously adaptable sauce that you will want to try with all sorts of food. As well as lamb, it is wonderful with crab cakes, grilled tuna or swordfish, pork tenderloin and chops. Try it on sandwiches filled with grilled vegetables and mild cheeses. Once you develop a taste for romesco sauce, you will think of many uses for it.

Makes 5 to 6 cups

1 large head garlic

2 cups plus 1 teaspoon olive oil

Kosher salt and freshly ground black pepper

2½ cups whole blanched
almonds (15 to 16 ounces)

Two 12-ounce jars or cans roasted red
peppers, drained (about 4 cups)

3 cloves garlic

¾ cup sherry vinegar

1 teaspoon sweet smoked paprika
(*pimentón de la vera dulce*)

½ teaspoon cayenne

½ teaspoon kosher salt

Freshly ground black pepper

1.   Preheat the oven to 350°F.

2.   Slice the top from the head of garlic to expose the cloves. Discard the tops. Put the garlic head, exposed side up, on a sheet of aluminum foil. Drizzle the garlic with 1 teaspoon of the olive oil and season with salt and pepper. Wrap the foil to form a loose package. Roast for about 45 minutes, or until the garlic is browned and tender.

3.   In a small saucepan, mix the remaining 2 cups of olive oil with the almonds, bring to a simmer over medium-low heat, and simmer for 12 to 15 minutes, or until the nuts are light brown. Adjust the heat to maintain the simmer. Strain the nuts from the oil to stop the cooking and let the nuts cool. Discard the oil.

4.   In a food processor fitted with the metal blade, roughly chop the red peppers, uncooked garlic cloves, and cooled almonds.

5.   Separate the head of roasted garlic into cloves. Discard the excess skins, but leave the garlic pulp encased in the skin. Squeeze the pulp from each clove into the food processor and pulse just until mixed with the chopped nuts and peppers.

6.   Add the vinegar, paprika, cayenne, and salt to the food processor and puree for about 1 minute, until well mixed but not smooth. The sauce should be chunky. Taste and season with salt and pepper.

7.   Use right away or transfer the sauce to an airtight container and refrigerate for up to 2 days.

chapter 4

Main Courses and Party Dishes

The original Barcelona had no main courses. For one thing, a true tapas bar is a place where you eat and drink before going to dinner; for another, we had all the food set up behind the bar, with no place to cook other than a toaster oven and a microwave. We debated for a long time about whether to add entrées. It meant outfitting a kitchen, hiring a chef, and changing the concept. On the other hand, people were settling in for dinner and asking, "Do you have a steak?" Worse still, a group of six would come in, five of whom were excited to try tapas and one of whom wanted an appetizer and a main course. It killed us to say, "No, sorry," and then watch them all leave.

We added entrées slowly and grudgingly—even now, our menu section for them consists of a core of five customer favorites and a few seasonal specials. We try to serve several fresh fish from the market every day and some stews or ragouts in colder weather. In the summer we feature a large composed salad for people eating healthfully. Still, there are rarely more than eight or nine entrées to go with the forty-plus tapas on the menu.

We differ from traditional restaurants in having a section on the menu called "For the Table." We wanted to do a traditional paella in the authentic thin-steel pans they

use in Spain; however, the smallest size makes enough food easily to feed two people. We decided to sell a "Paella for Two," and eventually people got the message and accepted the larger size. What they did with it was a bit of a surprise: rather than treat the paella as two entrées, they ordered a table full of tapas, finished them off, and then passed the paella around as a second "sharing" course.

Sasa, a voracious carnivore from his days in Argentina, thought it was criminal that our only sharing dish was full of fish, and so he proposed a true Argentine mixed grill, or *parillada*—complete with a big knife so people could serve themselves, French fries, and authentic chimichurri sauce, the South American catchall condiment for meat. At the beginning, Andy would jam the big, pointy knife into the board so that it went out to the table quivering. After

a few close calls with open-toed shoes, we went to laying the knife on the platter. The *parillada* was a big hit, and now we had large tables ordering paellas and *parilladas* and passing them both back and forth.

Today we have a true mix at our tables. Some customers have a meal of tapas, course after course; some have traditional appetizer-entrée meals; some share tapas first and then have individual entrées second; and some share tapas and then main dishes. It all feeds back into our philosophy: eat the way you want to—it's your night out, not ours. This idea translates to how you choose to entertain at home. You might want to start a meal with a few tapas, serve a menu of nothing but tapas, or host a paella party or blowout *parillada,* with a lot of people, a lot of food and wine, and a lot of fun. For more on a true Argentine *parillada,* turn to page 170.

Halibut with Puttanesca

We believe food should be simple, with the ingredients showcased at their natural best. We put more emphasis on the best execution of a straightforward concept than on intricate or multilevel flavors and presentation. This view of food makes an interesting tapa but a simple and unadorned main course.

This halibut is a dish with no pretension; use the best fish you can find and pair it with a great, classic, brightly colored puttanesca sauce. No awards for creativity here, but people lick their plates clean.

Serves 4

Four 6- to 7-ounce fillets of halibut

Kosher salt and freshly ground black pepper

5 tablespoons olive oil

1½ cups sliced red onion (1 to 2 onions)

3 teaspoons chopped garlic

¼ cup pitted Niçoise olives

2 teaspoons drained capers

¾ cup dry white wine

One 14-ounce Italian plum tomatoes

1 pound baby spinach leaves

1 tablespoon chopped flat-leaf parsley, for garnish

1. Preheat the oven to 425°F.

2. Season the halibut on both sides with salt and pepper.

3. In a large sauté pan, heat 2 tablespoons of the olive oil over high heat. When hot, cook the fish fillets for about 3 minutes on each side, or until opaque. Put the pan in the oven and cook until fish is just barely done.

4. Meanwhile, in another large sauté pan, heat 2 tablespoons of the remaining olive oil over high heat and cook the onion and 2 teaspoons of the garlic for 5 to 6 minutes, or until the onions are translucent but neither they nor the garlic browns. Add the olives and capers and cook, stirring, for about 2 minutes longer, or until heated through.

5. Add the wine and tomatoes with about half of their juice. Bring to a boil and cook for 4 to 5 minutes, or until sauce is thickened. Taste for seasoning. As the tomatoes cook, press on them with the back of a large spoon to extract more juices.

6. Meanwhile, rinse the spinach leaves with cool water and shake a little, but let a little water cling to the leaves.

7. Using a broad spatula, lift the fish from the pan and set aside. Add the remaining tablespoon of olive oil, the remaining teaspoon of garlic, and the spinach leaves. Cook for about 2 minutes, or until the spinach wilts and is heated through. It should still have some body and not be completely wilted. Season to taste with salt if needed.

8. Spoon about 1¼ cups of the puttanesca sauce onto each of 4 serving plates. Divide the spinach among the plates on top of the sauce and then add a fish fillet. Garnish with parsley and serve.

Chicken al Pimentos

This is one of our signature dishes. Chef Bill Rosenberg's wife is Sicilian, and one day she came in for lunch with her mother. Bill threw together some chunks of chicken, hot cherry peppers, and lemon and served them over pasta. Andy tried some and remembers asking, "What is that?"

"Oh, that's some Chicken Scarpiello for my Sicilian mother-in-law," Bill answered. Andy asked if he could run it as a special, minus the pasta, and it hasn't been off the menu since.

Hundreds of customers come in just for this chicken—some of them have it for dinner three or four times a week. It isn't a difficult recipe, but be sure to use high-quality chicken, such as Bell & Evans, and be careful not to overcook it.

Serves 4

Two 3½-pound chickens

1½ cups plus 4 tablespoons olive oil

3 russet potatoes, unpeeled, cut into sixteen ⅓-inch-thick slices

Kosher salt and freshly ground black pepper

2 tablespoons chopped garlic

4 cherry peppers, cored, halved, and seeded

2 cups chicken stock

¾ cup dry white wine

3 tablespoons freshly squeezed lemon juice, or more to taste

4 tablespoons unsalted butter

1. On a cutting board, turn a chicken upside down and, using a sharp knife, remove the legs where they meet the thighs. Reserve the legs for another use. Cut the wings at the second joint, leaving the third of the wing closest to the body intact. Reserve the wing tips.

2. Find the breastbone with your finger and put the blade of the knife along one side of the bone and work downward to release the meat from the ribs. Work the knife farther downward and into the joint to release the wing from the body.

3. Run the blade toward you, bend the thigh back at the joint, and cut through the thigh joint into the back, until the half chicken is freed from the bones. Turn the meat skin side down.

4. Find the thighbone and follow it with the blade of the knife. Make an incision along the bone from end to end. With your fingers, pull around the bone so that you can grab the back side of it. Pull up to free the bone further before cutting it free from one end. Scrape the bone with the knife blade to clean it of any meat. Hold the bone vertically and with a twisting motion pull it from the thigh.

5. Repeat this process with both sides of the chicken and with the second one until the chickens are boned and in two halves. Alternatively, you can ask the butcher to bone the chicken except for the wings.

6. Wrap the chicken in plastic wrap and refrigerate.

7. Preheat the oven to 450°F.

8. In a deep sauté pan, heat 1½ cups of the olive oil over medium heat for 10 to 12 minutes, or until it registers 425°F on a deep-fat thermometer, or until the oil bubbles when a cube of bread is dropped in it and the bread moves slightly in the oil.

9. Working in batches, fry the potatoes in the hot oil for 6 to 8 minutes, or until browned on each side. Using a slotted spoon, life the potatoes from the pan, drain on paper towels, and season with salt while still warm. Set aside, covered to keep them warm. Repeat, letting the oil regain its temperature between batches.

10. Remove the chicken from the refrigerator and season on both sides with salt and pepper.

11. In a large ovenproof sauté pan, heat 3 tablespoons of olive oil over medium-high heat. Sear the chicken, skin side down, for about 6 minutes, or until the skin is golden brown and crisp. You may have to do this in batches, depending on the size of the pan.

12. When the skin is completely brown, put the whole pan in the oven, with the skin side down.

13. Meanwhile, put the remaining 1 tablespoon of oil in a sauté pan and set the pan over high heat. Add the garlic and cook for about 2 minutes, stirring to prevent burning. Add the cherry peppers, chicken stock, wine, and lemon juice.

14. Bring the liquid to a boil and cook for 5 to 6 minutes, or until reduced by two-thirds. Season to taste with salt and pepper. When the chicken is cooked remove it from the pan and deglaze with the sauce, scraping the pan to remove any browned bits. Add the butter to the sauce, and return the roasted chicken, skin side up, and any accumulated juices to the sauté pan. Maneuver the chicken in the pan to keep as much of the skin as possible out of the sauce to keep it crispy and cook for about 2 minutes longer. Taste and add more lemon juice if necessary.

15. Put 4 potato slices on each of 4 serving plates. Put a half chicken next to the potatoes and then spoon about ¼ cup of the sauce over the chicken, with 4 cherry pepper halves in each serving. Serve immediately.

Roasted Suckling Pig with Thick-Cut Potatoes

This recipe calls for a cut-up pig, but if you have a large enough oven, or it's summertime and you are good with a grill, it is much more fun to roast the whole pig in one piece. Our chimichurri on page 171 is a great accompaniment to roast sucking pig. Save the pig's bones and use them to enrich stocks to be used for cooking beans or as a base for *cocido*.

Serves 8 to 10

One 20-pound suckling pig, cut into parts (legs separated from the body, backbone split, and ribs quartered)

2 cups chopped garlic (3 to 4 heads)

1½ cups sweet smoked paprika (*pimentón de la vera dulce*)

1 cup kosher salt

¼ cup freshly ground black pepper

6 russet potatoes, peeled and sliced lengthwise about ⅓ inch thick

1. Preheat the oven to 250°F.

2. Using a small, sharp knife, score the pig's skin all over with shallow crosshatch slashes.

3. In a medium mixing bowl, mix the garlic with the paprika, salt, and pepper and stir well. Rub this over the pig and work it into the slashes. (You should do this a day ahead of time. Refrigerate until about 1 hour before grilling.) Transfer the pieces of pig to 2 shallow roasting pans, skin side up. Cover with aluminum foil and roast for 5 hours.

4. Increase the oven temperature to 375°F.

5. Remove the foil from the pans and cook the pig for 2½ to 3 hours longer, or until the skin is crisp and the meat is cooked through, with the thickest parts of the pig registering 150° to 155°F on an instant-read thermometer. Some of the pig pieces will cook a little faster than others, but all will cook at approximately the same rate. Use your judgment about when to remove them from the oven. Transfer the pig pieces to cutting boards and leave the juices and fat in the pans.

6. Increase the oven temperature to 450°F.

7. Toss the potato slices in the pan juices and fat and then arrange them in a single layer in the pans. Season with salt and pepper and roast for 20 to 25 minutes, or until tender and crisp.

8. Meanwhile, slice the pig: Cut the ribs apart, remove the fillet from the backbone and slice. Slice the hams and pull the shank meat from the legs. If not using the head for decoration, pull the meat from the cheeks and upper brow.

9. Lay the sliced pork on a large platter and pile the ribs next to the meat. Surround the meat with the sliced potatoes and serve.

Churrasco

In South America, *churrasco* is a term for a variety of grilled steaks. Sasa had his mind set on the diaphragm skirt steak, one of the most flavorful and juicy cuts. Back in 1996, the only thing anybody used it for was fajitas, and it took us a while to get any kind of steak supply. Skirt steak now is on many bistro and Latin-fusion menus, and it costs as much as rib eye. We serve it *au naturel*, with classic Argentine chimichurri sauce: the oil, vinegar, and herb-based accompaniment to everything that comes off the grill in South America.

Serves 4

3 large sweet potatoes, peeled and each cut into 6 to 8 wedges

½ cup plus 3 tablespoons olive oil

2 teaspoons sweet smoked paprika (*pimentón de la vera dulce*)

¼ teaspoon cayenne

Kosher salt

3 cups olive or canola oil, for deep frying

Four 9-ounce skirt steaks, cut from the diaphragm

Freshly ground black pepper

1 tablespoon chopped garlic

1 pound baby spinach leaves, with a little water clinging to the leaves

About 1 cup Cilantro Chimichurri (recipe follows)

1. Preheat the oven to 425°F.

2. In a mixing bowl, toss the potato wedges with 2 tablespoons of the olive oil, the paprika, and the cayenne. Season to taste with salt.

3. Divide ½ cup of the remaining olive oil between 2 shallow roasting pans and tip the pans to coat them evenly with oil. Arrange the potato wedges in a single layer in each pan and roast for about 20 minutes, or until tender. Watch carefully to prevent burning.

4. In a deep sauté pan, heat the 3 cups of olive or canola oil for 10 to 12 minutes over medium heat. When the oil is hot, it will bubble when a cube of bread is dropped in it and the bread will move slightly in the oil.

5. Working in batches, fry the partially cooked sweet potato wedges for 5 to 7 minutes, or until slightly browned. Using a slotted spoon, lift the potatoes from the oil, drain on paper towels, and season with salt while still warm. Set aside, covered, to keep warm. Let the oil regain its temperature between batches.

6. Lightly spray the grates of a gas or charcoal grill with flavorless vegetable oil spray. Preheat the gas grill or prepare the charcoal grill so that the heating element or charcoal is hot. Alternatively, preheat the broiler.

7. Meanwhile, season both sides of the steaks with salt and pepper. Grill for about 5 minutes on each side, or until done to your desired degree of doneness. Let the steak rest for a few minutes.

8. Heat a large sauté pan over high heat and, when hot, pour in the remaining tablespoon of olive oil. Add the garlic and sauté for about 2 minutes, or until lightly browned. Add the spinach, season with salt, and cook for about 3 minutes, shaking the pan slightly, or until wilted.

9. Spoon ½ cup of chimichurri down the center of each of 4 serving plates. Divide the spinach among the plates and then put 5 to 7 potato wedges on each plate. Slice the steaks and set a few slices on top of the chimichurri. Serve immediately.

cilantro chimichurri

Every household in Argentina, Brazil, Uruguay, and Colombia has its own recipe for chimichurri sauce. The only common denominators are the oil, vinegar, and fresh herbs. Vary the amount of jalapeños or hot red pepper flakes, depending on how much heat you like. You will want to make this sauce often to serve with other meats, fish, and vegetables. It will keep overnight, but the cilantro will look a little drab after the sauce is refrigerated. You can revive it by stirring in a little fresh cilantro.

Makes about 2½ cups

1 cup chopped fresh
cilantro (about ¼ pound)

1 cup chopped fresh flat-leaf
parsley (about ¼ pound)

1 cup sliced scallion, both
white and green parts

1½ cups extra-virgin olive oil

¼ cup freshly squeezed
lime juice

3 tablespoons sherry vinegar

2 tablespoons chopped garlic

2 tablespoon chopped
fresh oregano

¼ cup diced jalapeño
pepper (2 to 4 jalapeños)
or hot red pepper flakes

Kosher salt

In a mixing bowl, stir together the cilantro, parsley, scallion, olive oil, lime juice, sherry vinegar, garlic, oregano, and jalapeño. Stir well and season to taste with salt. Serve at once.

Pepper-Rubbed Filet Mignon with Brandy Reduction and Crispy Onions

This is our most popular main course. It is sophisticated but simple at the same time. Peppered beef tenderloin, mashed potatoes, spinach, and onion rings—it's a Peter Luger's meal on a single plate. We won't tell if you make only the onion rings.

Serves 4

Garlic Confit

3 cloves garlic

¼ cup olive oil

Crispy Onions

2 large Spanish onions, shaved or very thinly sliced (preferably with a mandoline)

3 cups milk

5 cups canola oil

2 cups instant flour or cake flour

2 cups semolina flour

Pepper-Rubbed Filet Mignon

½ cup black peppercorns

12 cloves garlic

3 tablespoon dried rosemary

3 tablespoons kosher salt

9 tablespoons olive oil

Four 7-ounce filets mignons (beef tenderloin)

1 pound Yukon Gold potatoes

Kosher salt

1½ cups milk

2 tablespoons unsalted butter

1 tablespoon chopped garlic

1 pound baby spinach leaves, with a little water clinging to the leaves

Freshly ground black pepper

½ cup brandy

2 cups veal stock or 1 cup chicken stock and 1 cup beef stock

1. To prepare the filet mignon: In a spice grinder, grind the peppercorns, garlic, rosemary, and salt to a fine powder. Transfer to a small bowl and add 6 tablespoons of the olive oil, and mix well.

2. Rub both cut sides of the filets with the spice mixture. Transfer the meat to a shallow dish, cover with plastic wrap, and refrigerate for at least 8 hours and up to 2 days.

3. To prepare the confit: In a small saucepan, bring the garlic cloves and olive oil to a simmer over medium heat. Cook for 10 to 12 minutes, or until the garlic cloves are tender and lightly browned. Adjust the heat to maintain the simmer and watch carefully so that the garlic does not burn.

4. Transfer the garlic and oil to a container and let the oil cool a little. Cover and refrigerate for 2 to 3 hours, until chilled, and up to 3 days.

5. To begin preparing the crispy onions: Submerge the shaved onions in the milk and refrigerate for 2 to 3 hours.

6. Preheat the over to 450°F.

7. In a pot, cover the potatoes with cold water and add a handful of salt. Bring to a boil over high heat and cook for about 15 minutes, or until tender. Drain and return to the pot. Heat over very low heat for 3 to 5 minutes or until the potatoes dry out.

8. Meanwhile, in a saucepan, bring the milk to a simmer over medium-low heat.

9. Add the garlic cloves from the confit to the potatoes and mash with a potato masher or fork. Add the warm milk and the butter, mix well, and season to taste with salt. Cover to keep warm.

10. Take the meat from the refrigerator and scrape off the rub. Season lightly with salt.

11. In a large ovenproof sauté pan, heat 2 tablespoons of the remaining olive oil over high heat. Sear the meat for about 4 minutes on each side, or until lightly browned. Transfer the pan to the oven and roast for 8 to 10 minutes for medium-rare, or to the preferred degree of doneness. Remove the filets from the pan and set aside, covered, to keep warm.

12. Set the sauté pan over high heat and very carefully pour the brandy in the pan. The brandy could ignite, so pay close attention (if it does, remove the pan from the heat and the flames will subside quickly). Let the brandy cook for 2 minutes so that it reducues slightly. Add the stock and use a wooden spoon to scrape up any browned bits. Cook for 5 to 7 minutes, or until reduced by a third and thickened to a saucelike consistency. (The stock may take longer to reduce if you have mixed chicken and beef stock; veal stock reduces a little more quickly.)

13. To cook the onions: In a deep, heavy pot, heat the canola oil over medium heat until it reaches 350°F on a deep-fat thermometer. When the oil is hot, it will bubble when a cube of bread is dropped in and the bread will move slightly in the oil.

14. In a shallow dish, mix together the instant flour and the semolina flour.

15. Drain the onions and dredge with flour. Shake in a sieve or colander to remove any excess flour. Drop the onions into the hot oil and fry for 3 to 4 minutes, or until honey brown and crisp. Using a slotted spoon, lift the onions from the oil and drain on paper towels. Season to taste with salt while still warm.

16. In a sauté pan, heat the remaining 1 tablespoon of olive oil over high heat. Saute the chopped garlic for about 3 minutes, or until lightly browned. Add the spinach and cook for about 2 minutes, or until wilted. Season with salt and pepper to taste and set aside, covered, to keep warm.

17. Divide the potatoes among 4 serving plates. Spoon the spinach next to the potatoes. Rest a filet on the vegetables and ladle sauce over each one. Top each filet with onions and serve.

A VERY BIG STEAK

Our big steak was Andy's idea. We had seen similar cuts in Argentina on a recent trip, and he decided it would be pretty cool to offer a steak that was so big and so impressive our guests would gape as it was carried from the kitchen to a table. Chances were they would ask their waiter about it—and maybe even tell their friends. Buzz is a good thing in our business.

We turned to our old friend and meat supplier, Mark Berlin, who came up with a huge piece of meat, cut from the prime rib section all the way to the brisket, with the long bones extending from the meat. It looks like something Fred Flintstone would eat.

As soon as we started serving the steaks in December of 2007, they flew out of the kitchens, which was gratifying. No one would serve one of these behemoths at home, unless he or she had an oversized grill. They are meant for sharing, like many of our most popular entrées.

Because of their size, we had to design a wooden trencher just for them. This is not unusual for us, accustomed as we are to turning quirky ideas into reality.

We looked for well-marbled steak to make this dish work. "Marbeling" is the fat interspersed in the red meat, which gives it juiciness and flavor. The "cap fat" is the white part around the outside. Well-marbled meat "bastes" itself while cooking, which makes the cook's life easier.

When you grill any size steak, make sure that you season it well before putting it on the grill. Often we'll be asked what we did to the meat to make it taste so good— and the answer is, "Use enough salt and pepper." We grill the big steak until the center of the chop gives resistance to a firm push with the thumb. Then we let it rest for at least five minutes to allow the juices, which have been concentrated in the center by the heat, to redistribute themselves evenly throughout the steak.

Grilled Giant Prawns with Blood Orange

This dish came about as the result of a really great deal we got on the giant prawns we use to top our paella. All the restaurants were running prawn specials, and it was our Greenwich executive chef, Lisa Varnberg, who had the idea to use them in a winter salad. The dish caught on and has been a mainstay since. It sells well in the summer too, when people are in the mood for salads and grilled fish, but we have to substitute regular oranges.

Serves 4

2 cups blood orange juice
(about 4 oranges)

1 teaspoon sherry vinegar

1 red onion, sliced into very thin
rings (preferably with a mandoline)

1 bulb fennel, very thinly sliced
(preferably with a mandoline)

3 cups baby arugula leaves

½ bunch scallions, both white
and green parts, thinly sliced

Leaves from ½ bunch
fresh flat-leaf parsley

2 blood or navel oranges

12 jumbo high-quality shrimp (6–8
count), peeled and deveined

¼ cup olive oil

Kosher salt and freshly
ground black pepper

Juice of ½ lemon

3 tablespoons extra-virgin olive oil

1. In a small saucepan, bring the blood orange juice and vinegar to a boil over high heat. Cook for 8 to 10 minutes, or until reduced by half. Watch the sauce carefully so that it does not reduce too far. Set aside to cool or transfer to a lidded container and refrigerate for up to 2 days.

2. In a salad bowl, toss the onion, fennel, arugula, scallions, and parsley leaves together.

3. Slice the tops and bottoms off the oranges and then cut off the skin. Holding the oranges over a bowl to catch the juices, cut between the segments to separate them. Remove any membrane. Add the segments to the salad bowl.

4. Meanwhile, prepare a charcoal or gas grill so that the charcoal or heating element is medium-hot. Before putting the grates on the grill, lightly spray them with flavorless vegetable oil spray.

5. Rub the shrimp with oil and season lightly with salt and pepper. Grill for about 5 minutes and then turn them and grill for 3 to 5 minutes longer, or until the shrimp are pink and cooked through. Take care not to overcook them. Hold the shrimp on a plate until needed.

6. Squeeze the lemon juice over the salad and then drizzle with extra-virgin olive oil. Toss gently and season to taste with salt and pepper.

7. Mound the salad on 4 serving plates and then put 3 shrimp on each plate. Drizzle with the blood orange sauce and serve immediately.

Swordfish with Panzanella

A restaurant kitchen is no different from a home kitchen, and so we often find ourselves with day-old bread. We use it for bread crumbs, for croutons, and for this delicious Italian bread salad. Panzanella is best made with the juiciest summer tomatoes you can find and high-quality stale bread. The swordfish should be marinated in olive oil, which makes it easier to lift off the grill and keeps it moist. Be sure to cook the swordfish all the way through—rare swordfish is not tasty. When you think the fish is done, lift it and bend it with tongs: it should just break, not hold together.

Serves 4

Basil Oil

¾ cup olive oil

2 cups whole fresh basil leaves

1 clove garlic

¼ teaspoon kosher salt

Panzanella

2 pounds ripe tomatoes, halved horizontally and seeds squeezed out

½ red onion, thinly sliced

½ jalapeño pepper, stemmed, seeded, cored, and finely diced

8 fresh basil leaves, thinly sliced

2 tablespoons thinly sliced fresh flat-leaf parsley

Pinch of hot red pepper flakes

¾ cup tomato juice, or more as needed

3 teaspoons sherry vinegar

Kosher salt and freshly cracked black pepper

½ pound day-old or slightly stale country-style bread, crust removed and cut into 1-inch cubes

2 cloves garlic, chopped

3 tablespoons extra-virgin olive oil

2 tablespoons chopped fresh flat-leaf parsley

Swordfish

2 teaspoons extra-virgin olive oil

4 sprigs fresh thyme

4 sprigs fresh flat-leaf parsley

Kosher salt and freshly ground black pepper

Four 6-ounce center-cut fillets of swordfish, no thicker than ½ inch

Fresh basil sprigs, for garnish

1. To make the basil oil: In a blender, process the olive oil, basil leaves, garlic, and salt for about 2 minutes, until smooth and emulsified. Use immediately or refrigerate for up to 3 days in a tightly lidded container.

2. To prepare the panzanella: Preheat the oven to 425°F.

3. Core the tomatoes and cut into 1-inch dice. Transfer to a bowl and add the sliced onion, jalapeño, basil, parsley, pepper flakes, tomato juice, vinegar, and about 1 tablespoon of salt or to taste. Toss well and adjust the seasoning with pepper and more salt. The tomato salad is best on the second day but can be refrigerated for up to 4 days.

4. In another bowl, toss together the bread cubes, garlic, olive oil, and parsley. Season lightly with salt and pepper. Spread on a baking sheet and bake for 15 to 20 minutes, stirring and turning to encourage even browning, or until lightly browned and crisp. Remove from the oven, transfer to a large plate or platter to cool, and set aside.

5. To prepare the fish: In a shallow nonreactive dish, mix together the extra-virgin olive oil, thyme, and parsley. Season lightly with salt and pepper. Add the swordfish fillets and turn several times to coat. Cover and set aside at room temperature for up to 2 hours or in the refrigerator for 8 hours. (If it's a very hot day and your kitchen is warm, do not leave the fish at room temperature for more than an hour or so.)

6. Prepare a charcoal or gas grill so that the charcoal or heating element is medium-hot. Very lightly spray the grates with vegetable oil spray to prevent sticking. Alternatively, preheat the broiler.

7. Lift the fish from the marinade, let it drip off, and season the fish on both sides with salt and pepper. Grill for 4 to 5 minutes on one side. Turn over and grill for 2 to 3 minutes longer, or until the fish is opaque nearly all the way through.

8. Just before the fish is done, add the croutons to the tomato salad and toss well. There should be a lot of juice, but if not, add a little tomato juice. Taste and season with salt and pepper.

9. Cut the bottom out of a plastic 1-pint container to help form the salad on the plates.

10. Position the pint mold in the center of one of the 4 plates. Pack the panzanella salad into it, allowing juices to flood the plate. Lift off the pint mold and repeat on the remaining plates.

11. Rest a fish fillet on top of the salad and garnish each plate with a sprig of basil tucked behind the fish and a drizzle of basil oil.

PURVEYORS OF THE FINEST SEAFOOD

Just across Water Street from our South Norwalk office is a chilly warehouse where on any given day Alan Pagano, his brother Ralph, and Rick Drumgold work the phones. They sit at desks in an area that is slightly warmer than the rest of the facility, with large glass windows overlooking the cement cutting floor, where fish of all sizes are butchered, weighed, and packed for wholesale distribution. The phones never stop for these guys. Restaurants and markets from Fairfield County and beyond call constantly, and the Paganos fill orders as deftly as their workers strip a fish of its scales. The cutting floor and adjacent cold rooms smell of fresh fish and cold water. Men wear rubber boots and waterproof overalls as they work, necessary because of the water on the floor and the job of working with raw fish.

We're lucky to have Pagano's Seafood so close at hand. Alan has been running the business for some twenty years and knows his fish. A lot of the best comes to us. Our customers love seafood, and we like cooking it. What's paella without great shrimp and clams? How can we serve our Gambas al Ajillo without outstanding white or pink shrimp from South America or the Gulf Coast?

Pagano's makes sure we get what we need, and our chefs know to ask for "top of the trip" fish—which means the fish that are last caught before the fishing boat heads to shore. Still, as with any fish buying, not everything is available all the time. If the Paganos don't like the snapper one day, they will push grouper or striped bass. They get sardines flown in from Portugal on Thursdays, and we serve them that weekend. A few of our chefs like to take the guesswork out of the equation. They drive to Pagano's warehouse, pick out the fish they like, and throw them in their cars.

Home cooks can do a lot to ensure the fish they buy is as fresh as ours. First, find a fish counter with good turnover. You can usually tell by the number of customers lined up to buy fish, but you can also determine a lot by how the fish looks and how the area smells. Fish should be firm and moist, displayed on beds of clean chopped ice. Any whole fish should have bright eyes (never cloudy), firm, bright scales and reddish gills. The fish counter and the fish itself should smell of nothing but the sea. If there is a discernible "fishy smell," avoid that purveyor.

Lemon Sole with Crushed Peas and Vinaigrette

This is a springtime special, perfect for the first good peas of the season and light, fresh lemon sole. In Spain they love subtle white fish such as sole, hake, and cod, and we are lucky to be near New England's waters where these fish are shipped in daily. This sole dish is easy and requires only a short time to make.

Serves 4

Vinaigrette

1½ cups olive oil

⅓ cup sherry vinaigrette

¼ cup Dijon mustard

2 shallots, coarsely chopped

Kosher salt and freshly ground black pepper

Lemon Sole and Peas

Kosher salt

4½ cups fresh or frozen peas (about 5 pounds fresh peas in the pod)

1 tablespoon unsalted butter

2 shallots, thinly sliced (preferably with a mandoline)

Freshly ground black pepper

2 tablespoons chopped fresh marjoram or oregano

1 teaspoon olive oil

Four 6-ounce lemon sole or other flatfish fillets (such as fluke or flounder)

Juice of ½ lemon

Sea salt, for garnish

1. To make the vinaigrette: In a blender, puree the olive oil, vinegar, mustard, and shallots. Season to taste with salt and pepper and pulse to mix.

2. Use the vinaigrette right away or transfer to a lidded container and refrigerate for up to 2 days.

3. To prepare the fish and peas: Set a bowl of ice water near the stove. Fill a pot halfway with cold water, add 2 tablespoons of salt, and bring to a boil over high heat. Add the peas and cook for no longer than 2 minutes, or until they are bright green and beginning to turn tender. Drain the peas and immediately plunge them into the ice water to stop the cooking. When the peas are cold, drain.

4. Put 2½ cups of the peas in a blender and process until coarsely pureed. (The peas can be prepared up to this point 24 hours ahead of time and stored in a lidded container in the refrigerator.)

5. In a large sauté pan, melt 2 teaspoons of the butter over medium heat. Add the shallots, season to taste with salt and pepper, and sauté for 3 to 4 minutes, or until translucent but not browned.

6. Add the pea puree, whole peas, and marjoram to the pan and cook gently until heated through. Stir to mix the pureed peas with the whole peas. Taste and season with salt and pepper.

7. In another large sauté pan, heat the olive oil and remaining 1 teaspoon of butter over medium-high heat.

8. Season the fish fillets on both sides with salt and pepper and cook, skin side up, for 5 to 6 minutes, or until the edges of the fish are browned. With a large spatula, carefully turn the fillets and cook for 4 to 5 minutes longer, or until opaque and cooked through. Sprinkle the lemon juice over the fish.

9. Put about a cup of the peas in the center of each of 4 serving plates. Top the peas with a fish fillet and drizzle the vinaigrette around the plate. Drizzle any accumulated butter and lemon juice remaining in the sauté pan over the fish. Garnish each plate with sea salt and serve.

Grilled Sea Bass with Warm Salad of Fingerling Potatoes and Wax Beans with Broken Shallot Vinaigrette

This is a light, healthful dish that is best in summer, when fresh yellow wax beans and good new potatoes are available. Use black bass, if you can get it, or striped bass. Do not use Chilean sea bass, as the skin has an unpleasant taste. "Broken" vinaigrette means the oil and vinegar have separated, which is part of the messy charm of this dish.

Serves 4

Vinaigrette

2 tablespoons olive oil

2 cups sliced shallots
(8 to 10 shallots)

Kosher salt and freshly
ground black pepper

1½ cups chicken stock

1 cup sherry vinegar

¾ cup extra-virgin olive oil

Potato Salad

Kosher salt

1 pound wax beans, trimmed

1 pound fingerling potatoes

½ pint cherry tomatoes, halved

2 tablespoons chopped
flat-leaf parsley

Freshly ground black pepper

Sea Bass

Four 6- to 7-ounce fillets of
black bass or sea bass, skin
on, 2½ to 3 inches thick

Kosher salt and freshly
ground black pepper

2 teaspoons olive oil

1. For the vinaigrette: In a medium saucepan, heat the olive oil over medium-high heat. Add the shallots and sauté for about 8 minutes, or until tender and lightly browned. Season to taste with salt and pepper.

2. Pour the chicken stock, vinegar, and extra-virgin olive oil into the pot with the shallots and bring to a boil over high heat. Boil for 6 to 8 minutes, or until reduced by about a third. Remove from the heat, cover, and keep warm.

3. For the potato salad: Set a bowl of ice water near the stove. Fill a medium saucepan halfway with cold salted water and bring to a boil over high heat. Add the beans and cook for 3 to 4 minutes, or just until tender. Drain the beans and immediately plunge them into the ice water to stop the cooking. When the beans are cold, drain.

4. Put the potatoes in a pot and add enough cold water to cover by about 2 inches. Add plenty of salt and bring to a boil over high heat. Cook for 10 to 12 minutes, or until fork tender. Drain and, when cool enough to handle, slice each potato in half lengthwise.

5. In a large sauté pan over medium-high heat, warm the potatoes and beans with 2 tablespoons of the vinaigrette for 5 to 6 minutes, or until heated through. Add the tomatoes and parsley and toss to mix. Season to taste with salt and pepper.

6. For the sea bass: Lightly spray the grates of a gas or charcoal grill with flavorless vegetable oil spray. Preheat the gas grill or prepare the charcoal grill so that the heating element or charcoal is hot. Alternatively, preheat the broiler.

7. Season the fish on both sides with salt and pepper and rub the olive oil over both sides of the fish. Grill, skin side down, for 6 minutes. Turn and grill for 5 to 7 minutes longer, or until cooked through and the center of each fillet is opaque.

8. Spoon a quarter of the warm potato salad in the center of each of 4 serving plates. Lay a fish fillet, skin side up, on top and then ladle about 3 tablespoons of the vinaigrette over each serving.

Mussels and Clams a la Paulo

This terrific dish is a cross between a soup and a stew. It's a great addition to an asado as it tastes great eaten outdoors with some crusty bread for sopping up the juices. We learned how to make it from Sasa's friend Paulo from Portugal.

Serves 8

½ cup extra-virgin olive oil

1 sweet onion, such as Vidalia, cut into half-moons

8 cloves garlic, crushed

1 teaspoon red hot pepper flakes

1 pound ripe tomatoes, cored and diced

Sea salt

2 pounds littleneck clams

2 cups dry white wine

3 pounds Prince Edward Island or other high-quality mussels

1 bunch fresh cilantro, coarsely chopped

1. In a deep cast-iron pot with lid or a similar deep heavy saucepan, heat about ¼ cup of the oil over low heat. When hot, sauté the onion for 5 to 6 minutes, or until lightly browned and translucent. With a slotted spoon, remove the onion from the pan and set aside.

2. Add the remaining ¼ cup of the olive oil. When it is hot, sauté the garlic over medium-low heat for about 3 minutes, or until golden brown. Stir in the red pepper flakes and cook for 5 to 10 seconds.

3. Add the tomatoes and season to taste with salt. Raise the heat to medium-high, stir the tomatoes once, and then let them cook for 5 minutes without disturbing them.

4. Add the clams, cooked onion, and wine and stir once. Cover and cook for 4 to 5 minutes. Add the mussels and cook for 5 to 8 minutes longer, or until all the shellfish open. (Discard any that do not open.)

5. Add the cilantro and toss. Ladle the clams, mussels, and vegetables into shallow bowls. Drizzle each serving with olive oil and serve.

Double-Thick Pork Chops with Basque Peppers and Crushed Fingerling Potatoes

This dish is the antitapa. It's huge and designed for serious eaters. The flavors fit the Barcelona mold: pork is a Spanish staple, and the peppers are spicy, garlicky, and vinegar laced. It was developed by Pedro Garzon, our chef in New Haven and the one true Spaniard in the company. Although he was raised and educated in the States, his family owns an olive grove in the south of Spain, and his cooking is steadfastly authentic.

Harissa is a spicy hot pepper sauce originating in North Africa and sold at some supermarkets and also stores selling Middle Eastern and African foods. If you can't find it, substitute Asian-style red chili paste.

Serves 4

2 tablespoons harissa	4 double-boned loin pork chops, each about 1¾ to 2 inches thick	2 red bell peppers, seeded, cored, and julienned
2 tablespoons chopped fresh flat-leaf parsley	1 pound fingerling potatoes	2 green bell peppers, seeded, cored, and julienned
2 teaspoons ground cumin	Kosher salt	1 large Spanish onion, thinly sliced
1 teaspoon ground coriander	3 tablespoons extra-virgin olive oil	2 cups veal stock or 1 cup beef stock and 1 cup chicken stock
1 teaspoon aniseeds	2 tablespoons olive oil	
Freshly ground black pepper	2 tablespoons chopped garlic	

1. In a small mixing bowl, stir together the harissa, parsley, cumin, coriander, aniseeds, and ¼ teaspoon of pepper. Stir to make a paste.

2. Spread the paste over both sides of the chops. Wrap the chops in plastic wrap or put in a lidded container and refrigerate for at least 5 hours and up to 2 days.

3. Lightly spray the grates of a gas or charcoal grill with flavorless vegetable oil spray. Preheat the gas grill or prepare the charcoal grill so that the heating element or charcoal is hot.

4. Preheat the oven to 450°F.

5. Grill the pork chops for 8 to 10 minutes on each side. (They will not be cooked through.) Transfer to a shallow baking pan and bake in the oven for about 15 minutes.

6. Meanwhile, put the potatoes in a pot and cover with water. Season with salt and bring to a boil over high heat.

Boil for 8 to 12 minutes, or until tender. Drain and return the potatoes to the pot and cook over low heat for 2 to 3 minutes to dry out. With a potato masher or a fork, mash the potatoes with the extra-virgin olive oil. Season to taste with salt and pepper. Cover to keep warm.

7. In a large sauté pan, heat the olive oil over medium-high heat. When hot, cook the garlic for 3 to 4 minutes, stirring, until softened but not colored. Add the bell peppers and onion, season to taste with salt and pepper, and sauté for about 8 minutes, or until softened.

8. Add the stock, raise the heat to high, and cook for about 7 minutes, or until the liquid is reduced by half and the vegetables are very soft. The mixture will be moist and juicy.

9. Spoon about a quarter of the potatoes into the center of each of 4 serving plates. Put a pork chop on top of the potatoes and garnish with the peppers and onion.

Zarzuela

All seafood-loving cultures have a "kitchen sink" dish where they combine bits and pieces of whatever is fresh and available: *bouillabaisse* in France, *zuppa di pesce* in Italy, and *zarzuela* in Spain. Although we've suggested monkfish, clams, mussels, and scallops, feel free to substitute other seafood. The garlic, tomato, and high-quality fish stock are nonnegotiable.

Serves 4

3 tablespoons olive oil

1 pound monkfish or other firm-fleshed white fish (such as grouper or bass), cut into 1-inch chunks

8 large shrimp, peeled and deveined

2 tablespoons chopped garlic

8 large scallops

3 tablespoons sliced shallots (2 large shallots)

16 littleneck clams

16 Prince Edward Island or other high-quality mussels

½ pound cleaned calamari, cut into ½-inch-thick rings

2 teaspoons chopped fresh thyme

7 cups fish stock or a mixture of 4 cups chicken stock and 3 cups bottled clam juice

1½ cups dry white wine

2 cups chopped tomato

Kosher salt (optional)

1. In a Dutch oven or similar deep, wide pot, heat the olive oil over medium-high heat. When hot, season the monkfish with salt and pepper, and cook for about 3 minutes. Turn and cook for 3 about minutes longer, or until lightly colored.

2. Add the shrimp and garlic to the pot and cook for 2 to 3 minutes, stirring, or until the garlic starts to color. Add the scallops and shallots, cook for about 2 minutes, stirring, and then add the clams, mussels, calamari, and thyme.

3. Raise the heat to high, add the stock and wine, and bring to a boil. Boil for 6 to 7 minutes, or until the clams and mussels open. (Discard any that do not open.) Add the tomato, heat through, and season to taste with salt if necessary. (The seafood and broth tend to be salty, so you may not need any additional salt.)

4. Ladle the stew into 4 shallow bowls. Divide the fish and seafood evenly among the bowls. Serve immediately.

variation:

For a seafood stew called *romescado*, stir about 2 cups of Romesco Sauce (page 133) into the stew just before serving.

THE MEAT GUY

Mark Berlin, a big man with a ready smile, is a familiar sight at our restaurants. His company supplies us with meat and poultry, and when we deal with Mark we know we will get the best there is. There aren't too many guys like Mark left working in the business. Most restaurants rely on butchered, Cryovacked meat delivered from a conglomerate. We have a personal relationship with Mark, and it makes a difference.

If a chef runs out of beef tenderloin early on a Saturday night, Mark will jump into his truck and make a delivery before the customers know there's a problem.

Although Mark started his business in Norwalk not too far from our first restaurant, he now has a warehouse in nearby Bridgeport, from which he supplies more than seventy-five restaurants and markets throughout the state. He buys 90 percent of his meat from a single wholesaler based in New York called Westside Foods, and every day he or one of his guys goes to the Hunts Point Market in the Bronx. This kind of diligence means he can trace every piece of meat he sells back to its origin. It also means we get Sterling Silver beef, which is a brand graded at the very high end of choice, almost at the level of prime. Mark says that at any one time he has about $150,000 worth of meat in his warehouse. He also helps us out by storing our extra cases of Spanish olive oil there.

With the assistance of his wife, Rhonda, and a few experienced delivery men, Mark runs a tight ship. Still, he's always up for trying something new, as evidenced when he helped Andy figure out how to butcher the meat for our big steak (see page 146). As a master butcher, he wishes more of the meat he buys required more cutting, because he trusts his own skills most, but these days it tends to arrive already partially butchered into sections. Nonetheless, he and his team cut the meat to order at the warehouse, pack it, and ship it out the same day.

Mark starts work at 2:30 every morning, and his two vans and one truck are ready to hit the road for deliveries by 9:00. Their day ends at about 2:00 in the afternoon, when Mark goes home to rest up for the next day. He's in bed by 4:00 in the afternoon. We always get our meat nice and early and are ready to go when the first order comes into the kitchen.

That's service.

Home cooks usually have to choose from packaged cuts in the meat bins at the supermarket. Seek out fresh-looking meat with no visible moisture in the package. The meat should not look dried out or two-toned. If reddish liquid pools in a package of chicken, pass it by. This indicates that the poultry has been frozen, thawed, and refrozen.

When you buy beef, look for firm red meat (not bright red) with even marbling—streaks of fat running through the meat. While thick ropes of fat are not desirable, no visible fat will leave the meat dry and tasteless. Pork should be lighter pink than beef, and the streaks of fat should be creamy white, never yellowing or bright white. Lamb should be pink, firm, and lean with white external fat.

The people behind the meat counter at the supermarket are usually very helpful and will cut meat for you if you don't see what you like in the bin. Don't be afraid to push the bell and ask for assistance.

Rioja-Braised Lamb Shanks with Polenta and Garlic

Here is another winter favorite and one of our lamb dishes that sells well. We use the heavier rear shanks—they can weigh up to 20 ounces. The dish is a variant of one Andy used to do at Stars, as is the polenta. You can make polenta with water, stock, milk, or a combination of all three; just be sure there's enough salt in it when you start and resalt to taste. Finishing the polenta with plenty of butter keeps it from being "gummy."

Serves 4

Lamb Shanks

¼ cup olive oil

4 lamb shanks, each about 1 pound

2 carrots, peeled and coarsely chopped

2 ribs celery, coarsely chopped

1 yellow onion, coarsely chopped

1 head garlic, halved horizontally

4 cups veal or beef stock

3 cups chicken stock

3 cups dry red wine

2 bay leaves

1 teaspoon black peppercorns

Polenta

2 tablespoons olive oil

1 tablespoon chopped garlic

5 cups milk

1½ cups polenta

Sea salt and freshly ground black pepper

4 tablespoons unsalted butter

1 head escarole, quartered

1. To prepare the shanks: In a Dutch oven or similar deep, wide pot, heat the olive oil over medium-high heat and, when hot, sear the lamb shanks on all sides for 3 to 4 minutes a side. Be sure to sear all 4 sides of the shanks. Remove the shanks from the pot and set aside.

2. Put the carrots, celery, onion, and garlic in the pot and cook gently, stirring now and then, for about 12 minutes, or until the vegetables start to turn tender. Add the stock, wine, bay leaves, and peppercorns to the pot. Return the shanks to the pot and bring up to a boil over high heat.

3. Reduce the heat to medium-low so that the liquid simmers. Cover and cook for 2½ to 3 hours, or until the lamb is tender and can easily be pulled from the bones with your fingers. Adjust the heat to maintain a slow simmer.

4. Lift the shanks from the pot and set aside, covered, to keep them warm. Strain the liquid into another pot and skim the fat from the surface with a metal spoon. Discard the vegetables. Bring the strained liquid to a boil over high heat and boil for 15 to 20 minutes, or until the liquid is reduced by half and the consistency is saucelike. Return the shank to the sauce. The shanks and sauce can be prepared up to this point 2 days ahead. Store in tightly lidded containers.

5. To prepare the polenta: In a large saucepan, heat 1 tablespoon of the olive oil over medium heat and sauté the garlic for 3 to 5 minutes, or until slightly browned. Take care the garlic does not burn.

6.   Add the milk and bring to a rapid simmer over medium-high heat. Shake the polenta over it, whisking to prevent lumps from forming. Season well with salt and pepper. Lower the heat to medium-low and cook for about 20 minutes, stirring often, until thick and all the milk is absorbed. Remove from the heat and stir in the butter.

7.   In a large sauté pan, heat the remaining tablespoon of olive oil over medium-high heat. Rinse the escarole and shake gently so that some water clings to the leaves. Add the escarole and cook for 3 to 5 minutes, or just until wilted. Season with salt to taste.

8.   Reheat the lamb shank and sauce over medium heat until heated through. Season the sauce to taste.

9.   Spoon about a quarter of the polenta into each of 4 shallow bowls or onto 4 plates. Top with escarole and then a lamb shank. Ladle about a cup of the sauce over the shank and serve.

the barcelona cookbook

Peruvian Steak Salad

When Lisa, the executive chef at our Greenwich restaurant, first ran this salad as a special, she put purple potatoes in it and called it "Peruvian." The combination of grilled marinated steak and crunchy salad was a hit, and it stayed on the menu long after purple potatoes were out of season. When customers now ask what makes the salad "Peruvian," we deftly change the subject.

Serves 4

Dressing

1 cup balsamic vinegar

¾ cup soy sauce

1 teaspoon honey

Pinch of hot red pepper flakes

Freshly ground black pepper

Salad

2 plum tomatoes, peeled and seeded, firm flesh chopped

1 red bell pepper, seeded, cored, and thinly sliced

1 poblano or green bell pepper, seeded, cored, and thinly sliced

½ jícama, peeled and julienned (preferably with a mandoline)

½ English cucumber, julienned (preferably with a mandoline)

½ red onion, thinly sliced

Four 8-ounce pieces skirt steak, trimmed of excess fat

Kosher salt and freshly ground black pepper

2 heads romaine lettuce, coarsely chopped

Juice of ½ lemon

3 tablespoons extra-virgin olive oil

Fresh cilantro sprigs, for garnish

1. To make the dressing: Whisk together the vinegar, soy sauce, and honey. Season with the pepper flakes and black pepper. Set aside until needed or cover and refrigerate for up to 5 days. Whisk or shake well before using.

2. To make the salad: In a mixing bowl, toss together the tomatoes, red bell pepper, poblano pepper, jícama, cucumber, and onion.

3. Prepare a gas or charcoal grill so that the heating element or charcoal is hot.

4. Season the steaks on both sides with salt and pepper. Grill for 4 to 5 minutes on each side, until medium-rare or cooked to your desired degree of doneness. Set aside to rest for about 10 minutes.

5. Divide the lettuce among 4 salad plates. Drizzle lemon juice over each plate and then drizzle each with a little extra-virgin olive oil.

6. Spoon about 3 tablespoons of the dressing over the bowl of mixed vegetables and toss to mix. Spoon equal amounts of the vegetables over the lettuce.

7. Slice the steaks on the bias into strips ½ inch wide by ¾ inch long, cutting nearly to the edge of the steak but leaving each piece intact. Wrap the steak around the mound of vegetables to resemble a crown. Garnish each plate with a cilantro sprig.

BIG PARTIES

The best way to give a party is to prepare a selection of easy or make-ahead tapas and spread them out on a buffet. Serve your favorites or those that appeal to you for one reason or another. We suggest a tapas lineup such as:

- Roasted Olives (page 29)

- Tuna Tartare with Yuca Chips (page 34)

- Roasted Chickpea Puree with Cumin-Toasted Pita Chips (page 54)

- Fire-Roasted Peppers with Boquerones (page 66)

- Wild Mushrooms with Herbed Cheese (page 90)

- Crab Cakes (page 97)

- Empanadas with Smoked Pepper Sauce (page 98)

Let people help themselves to the first half of the meal and then bring the paella, parillada, cocido, or roasted pig to the table and serve everyone family style. Set big, icy pitchers of sangria on the table and offer other cocktails, such as mojitos, caipirinhas, and blood orange margaritas. And of course lots of wine. We love Spanish wines, and you can't go wrong pairing them with these dishes. Read about some of the best Spanish wines on page 6.

Put some good music on the iPod—we like American jazz, blues, Brazilian bossa nova, and British rock.

To aid you further in your planning, you can experience a real Sunday afternoon asado (Argentine barbecue or grill) that Sasa gave for a group of friends on page 166. And if you are interested in tapas-only parties, turn to pages 60 and 61 for two menus for surefire fiestas!

ASADOS

Since the time Sasa was a young boy living in Buenos Aires, Argentina, he has been crazy about the Argentine tradition of the weekend *asado*. Roughly translated, an *asado* is a backyard barbecue or cookout, but as Barrett Hickman (one of Sasa's pals who traveled to Argentina extensively) says, comparing an *asado* to a typcial American barbecue is like comparing an ordinary church service to the Vatican's Easter celebration.

Argentinean *asado* cooks are uncompromising about the quality of the food and the care it demands, but their attitude toward the event is always spiked with good humor and great fun. Let's face it, an asado is a way of life.

The party may begin on a weekend evening and carry on long into the wee hours, with ample food and wine through the night. The party may also begin on Sunday afternoon and last well into the evening.

As our friend Jeff Giannone told us, when he wakes up on Sunday mornings he starts planning the menu and the guest list for the afternoon *asado*. It's our social equivalent of the age-old practice of sitting around the campfire, he says.

Asado grills are always fired by wood. In Sasa's Connecticut backyard, he relies on oak or another readily accessible hardwood. The grill is large but not fancy. It's fashioned by hand from bricks and a stationary grill rack that sits about five inches above the fire pit. The heat is controlled by the banked embers once the fire dies down. Cooking over the low embers means slow cooking—which is the point for an *asado*. We like the meat, poultry, fish, and vegetables cooked long and slow. This allows them to caramelize gently to bring out every flavor nuance and note, without any charred flavor.

In Buenos Aires and other Argentine cities, similar grills are found in front and back yards everywhere. Makeshift grills are assembled on street corners and in parks for impromptu *asados*. The tantalizing aroma of grilling meat fills the air, especially on weekends, when families and friends gather for the traditional ritual.

Anything goes at an *asado*, as long as it can be cooked over a low fire. We grill beef, pork, lamb, chicken, duck, and game, which are then served with chimichurri sauces. We carefully tend whole fish on the grill, as well as shellfish. Vegetables and some fruits are grilled to accentuate their natural sugars and render them full flavored and juicy.

Brussels sprouts are not grilled but cooked in the kitchen. They are sautéed in a little olive oil with sliced garlic.

When Sasa and his wife hosted this asado, the tomatoes from the local farmers' market were just perfect, and we cut red, yellow, and green "zebra" tomatoes into slices, layered them with fresh basil leaves, and then dressed them with extra-virgin olive oil and a touch of balsamic vinegar.

Meats on the grill include porterhouse steaks, lamb chops, New York strip, whole chickens, sweet sausage, sweetbreads, blood sausage, rabbit, and duck. Let the meat reach room temperature before grilling it and then cook it long and slow, until it is done to perfection.

Accompanying the grilled foods and the salads are platters of Spanish cheeses, olives, and cured meats. We serve these with the best bread we can buy, looking for freshly baked, crusty loaves, usually from a local baker.

For the roasted red bell pepper salad, we roasted the bell peppers on the grill until the outside charred just slightly, and then we let them steam in a covered bowl. After peeling the peppers, we tore them into 3 to 4 pieces and tossed them with extra-virgin olive oil, a touch of balsamic vinegar, and thinly sliced flat-leaf parsley. Finally, we seasoned the peppers to taste with sea salt.

The salads for the party included a German potato salad with marinated vadalia onion (no mayonnaise, but olive oil and vinegar instead) and a bean salad made with fava beans, kidney beans, chickpeas, and black-eyed peas tossed with chopped red onion, red bell peppers, and jalapeños dressed with extra-virgin olive oil, wine vinegar, lots of fresh herbs, and salt.

Portobello mushrooms, zucchini, eggplant, and asparagus are all grilled alongside the meat. They are first brushed with olive oil and seasoned with sprinklings of salt.

Accompanying the grilled foods are salads and other simple preparations, such as the Mussels and Clams a la Paulo (page 153), and cold soups such as the Barcelona Gazpacho (page 42). All kinds of tapas are welcome too. Friends and family members bring their favorites, and everyone pitches in to help. And, of course, we serve wine and perhaps a few cocktails to keep the party lively and play lots of good music to enhance the celebratory mood.

One Sunday afternoon Sasa gathered his good friends and family for an *asado* in his leafy backyard to feast on slow-grilled meats and vegetables and have a great time.

main courses and party dishes

Parillada

Once we started offering main courses and putting paella on the menu, we noticed that quite a few tables used the paella to continue a "sharing" meal. To accommodate a table of six, where five were sharing the paella and one wanted steak, Sasa had the idea to offer a version of an Argentine *asado*: a meal consisting of course after course of different meats, right off the grill. In Argentina, they call these grilled meat *parillada*.

We couldn't find the right plate to serve the meat on, and so we went to the lumberyard, bought a bunch of cherry planks, rented a router, and made our own. We started serving the *parillada* with a knife slammed point down and quivering in the board. After a few knives fell into customers' laps and on their feet, we stopped that practice. The offerings change from time to time: pork, lamb, chicken, sausage—but there is always a big sirloin steak and at least three other meats, hot off the grill. Chimichurri is the classic accompaniment to meat throughout South America and is made in as many different ways as there are people to make it. For our *asado*, we like this spicy red sauce, but you might prefer a milder chimichurri such as the green one on page 143. In Argentina, an *asado* can take up to four hours of eating and drinking . . . it's the best part of life. We suggest you divide the meal in three courses: chicken, sausage and lamb, then steak.

Serves 8

Two 1- to 1½-pound free-range poussins or 1 rabbit

Kosher salt and freshly ground black pepper

8 links sweet Italian sausage or chorizo

8 T-bone lamb chops

Two 2-inch-thick choice or prime porterhouse steaks

Sasa's Argentine Chimichurri, for serving (recipe follows)

1. Lightly spray the grates of a gas or charcoal grill with flavorless vegetable oil spray. Preheat the gas grill or prepare the charcoal grill so that the heating element or charcoal is hot. If your grill is not large, you might need to use two grills. All of the following steps should be done the same way: when the individual meats are done, transfer them to a board to rest, making sure to catch all the juices. Keep the meats covered with foil as the longer-cooking items finish. Let the last item (probably the steaks) rest a few minutes before serving.

2. Split the chickens or game hens and remove the backbones. (If using rabbits, remove the backbones and split the rabbits in half.) Season with salt and pepper.

3. Grill the poultry for 8 to 12 minutes on each side, or until firm to the touch and cooked through. (If cooking rabbits, grill for them for 10 to 12 minutes on each side, or until firm to the touch.) When cooked, move to a cool part of the grill or remove from the grill and transfer to a platter, covered with foil to keep it warm.

4. Grill the sausage for 7 to 9 minutes on each side, or until cooked through. When cooked, move to a cool part of the grill or remove from the grill and transfer to a platter, covered with foil to keep it warm.

5. Season the lamb with salt and pepper, and grill for 10 to 12 minutes on each side for medium-rare, or until it reaches the desired degree of doneness. When cooked, move it to a cool part of the grill or remove from the grill and transfer to a platter, covered with foil to keep it warm.

6. Season the steaks with salt and pepper, and grill for 8 to 10 minutes on each side for medium-rare meat, or until done to the desired degree of doneness.

7. Let the steaks rest for about 5 minutes and separate the sirloin and the fillet from the center bone. Slice and arrange the slices and the bone on a large serving platter.

8. Slice the racks of lamb to separate the chops. Place on the serving platter with the steak and sausages.

9. Take the poultry from the grill and cut into quarters by separating the legs and thighs from the breasts. (Cut the rabbits into quarters by cutting through the rib cage.) Transfer to the platter.

10. Sprinkle all the meats with sea salt, and serve with the chimichurri sauce on the side.

sasa's argentine chimichurri

This recipe is—of course—made the way Sasa's mother makes it. It's typical of chimichurri made in Argentina, although it has a little Hungarian influence too, in the amount of paprika. However, we call for Spanish paprika instead of Hungarian. Make sure not to use smoked paprika. Double the recipe for more sauce.

Makes about 1½ cups

1 cup chopped fresh flat-leaf parsley leaves

4 tablespoons chopped fresh oregano

¾ cup extra-virgin olive oil

¼ cup red wine vinegar

3 tablespoons sweet Spanish paprika (not smoked)

2 tablespoons balsamic vinegar

1 tablespoon hot red pepper flakes

6 cloves garlic, minced

Kosher salt and freshly ground black pepper

1. In a nonreactive mixing bowl, mix together the parsley, oregano, olive oil, red wine vinegar, paprika, balsamic vinegar, pepper flakes, and garlic. Season to taste with salt and pepper. Add more vinegar to taste. This should be vibrant. Use at once or cover and refrigerate for up to 2 months.

2. If you store the chimichurri, refresh it with a little chopped parsley, minced garlic, oil, vinegar, and salt before using it.

Paella Barcelona

We have made this paella thousands of times, but every one is still different. Paella is difficult to make in a restaurant—it should be made to order, cooked slowly on top of the stove, and served as soon as it is ready. We do all three of these, but we have to cheat and put it in the oven, since we just don't have the burner space to make ten at once.

Good paella is heavy on sofrito (the fragrant sauce made with peppers, olive oil, tomato paste, and garlic) and light on saffron. Great paella is all about the rice and not about the toppings. When you make paella the first time, taste the rice at regular intervals and don't worry about some sticking to the pan. That's the best part.

You can purchase paella seasoning at some supermarkets and specialty stores, particularly those selling Spanish products, or make your own, as in this recipe.

Serves 8 to 10

Paella Spice

4 teaspoons ground cumin

4 teaspoons sweet smoked paprika (*pimentón de la vera dulce*)

2 teaspoons ground turmeric

2 teaspoons ground coriander

½ teaspoon saffron threads

Paella

3 red bell peppers, seeded, cored, and coarsely chopped

3 green bell peppers, seeded, cored, and coarsely chopped

2 Spanish onions, coarsely chopped

5 tablespoons olive oil

¼ cup chopped garlic

1 tablespoon sweet paprika

3 tablespoons tomato paste

1 cup dry white wine

¾ teaspoon saffron threads

5 cups fish or chicken stock

2½ cups sliced smoked Spanish chorizo (about 1 pound)

3½ cups chunks boneless chicken thighs, with the skin (from 5 to 6 thighs)

Kosher salt and freshly ground black pepper

2½ cups Calasparra rice

8 large shrimp

18 littleneck clams, scrubbed

20 Prince Edward Island or other high-quality mussels, cleaned and scrubbed

2 tablespoons extra-virgin olive oil

1. To make the paella spice: Pulse the cumin, paprika, turmeric, coriander, and saffron in a spice grinder. Use right away or store in an airtight container for up to 1 month.

2. To make the paella: In a food processor fitted with the metal blade, process the bell peppers and onions until they resemble chunky applesauce.

3. In a saucepan set over medium heat, heat 2 tablespoons of the olive oil and, when hot, sauté 1 tablespoon of the garlic for 2 to 3 minutes, or until slightly browned. Add the pureed vegetables and paprika and bring to a simmer. Stir frequently as the mixture reaches the simmering point.

4. Add the tomato paste, white wine, and ¼ teaspoon of the saffron threads and simmer for 15 to 20 minutes, or until the liquid is reduced by half and the vegetables are tender. Cover and keep the sofrito warm until needed. If not using it right away, refrigerate in a container with a tight-fitting lid for up to 2 days.

5. In a large saucepan, bring the stock and remaining ½ teaspoon of saffron threads to a boil over high heat. Reduce the heat to low and simmer for about 15 minutes, or until the saffron has flavored and colored the stock.

6. Preheat the oven to 450°F.

7. Heat a paella pan or similar shallow pan measuring at least 12 inches across over medium heat. Add the remaining 3 tablespoons olive oil and the remaining 3 tablespoons garlic and sauté for 2 to 3 minutes. Add the chorizo and cook for 4 to 5 minutes, or until the fat is rendered and the sausage is slightly browned.

8. Season the chicken with salt and pepper and sauté for 6 to 7 minutes, or until lightly browned on all sides.

9. Add the rice, stir well, and sauté for 2 to 3 minutes. Add the paella spice and stir well. Stir the sofrito (pureed vegetables) into the pan and continue to cook for 4 to 5 minutes before adding the saffron-flavored stock. Bring to a boil over high heat.

10. Arrange the shrimp, clams, and mussels in the pan in a pleasing pattern. Cover with aluminum foil and transfer the paella pan to the oven. Cook for 15 minutes and then remove the foil. Cook for 10 to 15 minutes longer, or until the rice is tender and has absorbed the liquid.

11. Drizzle the paella with the extra-virgin olive oil and serve.

Cocido

As with the paella on page 172, this is a dish that serves a crowd and takes several hours to cook. A *cocido* is a stew, made with chickpeas and a combination of different meats and sausages. It is especially popular in the central regions of Spain, where meat reigns.

Serves 10 or more

Braise

3 tablespoons olive oil

One 3½-pound chicken, cut into 8 pieces (halve the breasts if large, for 10 pieces)

Kosher salt and freshly ground black pepper

One 3-pound beef brisket

3 pounds country-style pork spareribs

Five 4-inch links smoked chorizo or other sausage (such as butifarra, morcilla, or sweet Italian sausage)

2 cups sliced carrots (about ½ pound; 3 to 4 carrots)

1½ cups chopped celery (about ½ pound; 3 to 4 ribs)

1 Spanish onion, quartered

1 head garlic, halved

8 cups chicken stock

2 cups dry white wine

¼ pound flat-leaf parsley stalks (about 1 cup)

8 sprigs fresh thyme

8 black peppercorns

5 bay leaves

Cocido

1 pound fingerling potatoes

1 bulb fennel, cored and quartered

2 small turnips, peeled and quartered

1 head savoy cabbage, cored and cut into 6 wedges

One 15½-ounce can chickpeas, drained

2 Spanish onions, quartered

3 to 4 carrots, peeled and sliced

3 to 4 ribs celery, sliced

Serving

1 round loaf rustic country-style bread

Cornichons

Dijon mustard

1. To prepare the braise: In a large Dutch oven, heat the olive oil over medium-high heat.

2. Season the chicken with salt and pepper and brown on all sides, 5 to 8 minutes. Remove from the pot and set aside.

3. Season the brisket with salt and pepper and brown on all sides, 10 to 12 minutes. Remove from the pot and set aside.

4. Season the ribs with salt and pepper and brown on all sides, 8 to 10 minutes. Remove from the pot and set aside.

5. Sear the chorizo until lightly colored on one side and a little fat has been rendered.

6. Add the carrots, celery, onion, and head of garlic to the pot and sauté with the chorizo for about 5 minutes, or until the vegetables begin to soften. Pour the stock and wine into the pot and deglaze by scraping up any browned bits with a wooden spoon. Add the parsley, thyme, peppercorns, and bay leaves and bring to a boil over high heat.

7. Return the chicken, brisket, and pork ribs to the pot, reduce the heat to low, and cook at a low simmer for 2½ to 3 hours, or until the brisket is fork tender. Adjust the heat to maintain the simmer.

8. Using a slotted spoon, remove the meat from the pot and transfer to a platter.

9. Strain the broth through a sieve into another pot (or into a bowl and then return it to the original Dutch oven) and, using a metal spoon, skim the fat from the surface. Discard the vegetables.

10. To prepare the *cocido*: Add the potatoes, turnips, fennel, cabbage, chickpeas, onions, carrots, and celery to the pot with the broth. Bring to a boil and then reduce the heat to low. Simmer for 15 to 20 minutes, or until the potatoes are tender, skimming the surface regularly.

11. Meanwhile, slice the brisket and chorizo and separate the ribs.

12. Using a slotted spoon, remove the vegetables from the pot and transfer to a soup terrine or similar serving dish.

13. Season the broth with salt and pepper to taste. Ladle 4 cups over the vegetables.

14. Arrange the sliced meats, chicken pieces, and ribs on the serving platter and ladle about 2 cups of the strained broth over them.

15. Serve the meat on a platter with the broth on the side. Provide every diner with a plate and bowl and serve with bread, cornichons, and mustard.

chapter 5

Desserts

Our desserts are a mixture of Spanish and American. Clearly the flan and the churros are classic Iberian, whereas the Chocolate Indulgence and the Fruit Crisp are all-American. The Indulgence is by far our top seller—chocolate lovers are a loyal group—and the crepes filled with *dulce de leche*, the *churros*, which are dipped in thick liquid chocolate, and the flan, are close seconds. All lend themselves to entertaining at home and are simple enough to follow a tapas party, where flavors and textures are many and varied.

None of our desserts is hard to make. We don't have separate pastry kitchens in our restaurants but instead assemble the desserts at the cold tapas station. This is not unlike the reality of a home kitchen!

The Spanish like sweet, sticky pastries and liqueur-soaked cakes with creamy sauces. They often serve ice cream with fruit for dessert (and the fruit frequently is canned peaches packed in thick syrup, a treat not to be scoffed at in Spain). At the high-end restaurants in Spain desserts are as complicated and sophisticated as anywhere in the world, but at most restaurants, as at ours, they are a simple affair.

Cranberry-Orange Biscotti with Manchego Cheese

We're not sure why we started making biscotti. Like all Italian items on the menu, these, we assume, were introduced by Bill Rosenberg, who was one of our first chefs—especially since they are a particularly good version. Biscotti are very easy to make and are very tolerant. They actually get two bakings, so don't panic if they seem undercooked when you cut them into slices. You can play with the recipe as well: add almond extract, if you prefer, or dip them into melted dark or white chocolate when they cool. This recipe makes dozens of biscotti, but we don't recommend you make them all at once since the dough freezes very well for up to one month and you can make the rest later. Once baked, they keep for about a week in a tightly covered container.

Makes about 8 dozen biscotti

2 oranges

2¾ cups all-purpose flour

1 teaspoon baking powder

1 teaspoon salt

3 large eggs

1 cup sugar

2 teaspoons orange blossom water or orange-flavored liqueur, such as Grand Marnier

1 cup olive oil

1½ cups dried cranberries

6 to 8 ounces Manchego, Nevat, or Tetilla cheese, for serving (see page 107)

1. Preheat the oven to 325°F. Line a baking sheet with parchment paper.

2. With a vegetable peeler, peel the orange part of the skin (the zest) from the oranges. Leave the bitter white pith on the fruit. Slice the zest into thin strips and set aside.

3. In a mixing bowl, whisk together the flour, baking powder, and salt. Set aside.

4. In the bowl of an electric mixer fitted with the paddle attachment and set at medium speed, blend the eggs, sugar, orange blossom water, and olive oil until well mixed.

5. Slowly stir the flour mixture into the wet ingredients, mixing at low speed with the paddle attachment or by hand with a rubber spatula. When the mixture is well blended, stir in the orange zest strips and the cranberries.

6. Lightly spray a large sheet of parchment paper with flavorless vegetable oil to wrap the logs of dough you will form. Set aside.

7. Turn the dough out onto a lightly floured surface and work briefly so that the dough holds together. Divide the dough into quarters. Roll each in the parchment paper, using the paper as a guide, into a log approximately 12 inches long and about 1 inch in diameter. As one log is rolled, remove it from the parchment and roll the next. Wrap 2 of the logs in more parchment or wax paper and then in plastic wrap and freeze for up to 1 month.

8. Put the 2 remaining logs on the baking sheet lined with more parchment paper and bake for about 13 minutes. Rotate the baking sheet in the oven and bake the logs for 5 to 10 minutes longer, or until the logs are lightly browned and a toothpick inserted in the center of one of them comes out clean. Let the logs cool on wire racks for at least 20 minutes. Leave the oven on while the logs cool and leave the parchment paper on the baking sheet.

9. Using a serrated knife, slice the logs on the diagonal into ½-inch-thick slices. Lay the cookies on the baking sheet lined with parchment paper.

10. Turn off the oven and let the biscotti dry out in the oven for 45 to 60 minutes, or until dry, crispy, and lightly browned.

11. Cool the biscotti on wire racks and, when completely cool, serve with the cheese. The cookies can be stored in a container with a tight-fitting lid for up to 1 week.

Chocolate Indulgence

Here is yet another recipe from Bill Rosenberg, a prolific chef. When this went on the menu back in 1997, Jean-Georges Vongerichten was getting a lot of press for his warm Valrhona chocolate cakes, and we were accused of copying his creation. This was probably true, but oh, well—it tastes great.

The recipe is designed to be reheated in the microwave, which is a great trick for dinner parties. Just pop the cakes in long enough to get the surfaces good and hot, top with cold ice cream, and serve.

Serves 8

1 pound bittersweet or semisweet chocolate, coarsely chopped

1 cup (2 sticks) salted butter

½ cup sugar, plus 1 to 2 tablespoons for the raspberries (optional)

1 tablespoon pure vanilla extract

¾ cup hazelnut praline paste or Nutella

6 large eggs, lightly beaten

One 1-pound bag frozen unsweetened raspberries

2 pints vanilla ice cream, for serving

1. Preheat the oven to 350°F.

2. In the top of a double boiler set over simmering water on medium-high heat, melt the chocolate, butter, ½ cup sugar, and vanilla. Stir occasionally with a wooden spoon. It will take 10 to 12 minutes for the chocolate to melt. Whisk for 5 to 7 minutes longer, or until the butter and sugar melt and the mixture is incorporated. Alternatively, melt the chocolate, butter, sugar, and vanilla in the microwave.

3. Remove the top of the double boiler from the heat and whisk in the hazelnut paste until blended. Whisk in the eggs, one at a time.

4. Spray eight 4-ounce aluminum foil baking cups (doubling them up is a good idea to make them easy to handle and so that they hold their shape) or similar containers such as ramekin with flavorless vegetable oil spray. Ladle the batter into the cups so that they are three-quarters full. Transfer the filled cups to a shallow baking pan or baking sheet and bake for 30 to 35 minutes, or until firm and the tops crack a little.

5. In a food processor fitted with the metal blade, puree the raspberries. Sweeten with 1 or 2 tablespoons of sugar if desired. Strain the puree through a fine-mesh sieve into a small bowl.

6. Spoon about ¼ cup of the raspberry puree into the center of each of 8 serving plates.

7. Run a dull kitchen knife around the cups to loosen the warm cakes. Invert them on the raspberry puree. Top each cake with vanilla ice cream and serve.

Crepas Salguero

We have a friend named Jeff Salguero who invested in one of the restaurants and whose family is from Uruguay. He goes to South America regularly, and for years, every time he came back, he would ask why we didn't have *pancakes de dulce de leche* on the menu. *Dulce de leche*, or milk caramel, is the dessert ingredient of choice all over Latin America, and crepes filled with *dulce de leche* and whipped cream are as common in Uruguay as apple pie is in the United States.

Finally, to make Jeff stop asking, we put the crepes on the menu at the Greenwich location and named the dessert after him. It took only a few months before customers demanded it at all the other restaurants. That was five years ago. It's not going anywhere, and Jeff still eats it when he comes for dinner.

Serves 8

Crepes

Two 12-ounce cans condensed milk

1 cup all-purpose flour

1 cup milk

½ cup water

1 large egg

1 tablespoon butter, melted

2 tablespoons sugar

Chocolate Sauce

1 pound semisweet or bittersweet chocolate, coarsely chopped, or 1 pound semisweet or bittersweet chocolate chips

1½ cups heavy cream

½ cup brewed coffee

2 cups whipped cream, sweetened if desired, for serving

2 pints vanilla ice cream, for serving

1. To make the *dulce de leche*: Remove the labels from the cans of condensed milk and submerge them in a large pot filled with water. Bring to a boil over high heat, reduce to a rapid simmer, and simmer for about 4 hours. Add water as needed. Check often to make sure the cans are always covered with water by at least 1 inch; otherwise they could explode. Remove the cans from the water and let them cool.

2. In a large mixing bowl, mix together the flour, milk, water, egg, and melted butter. Whisk by hand for about 2 minutes. Add the sugar and whisk for about 2 minutes longer. Strain through a fine-mesh sieve into a bowl and let the crepe batter rest for about 20 minutes.

3. To make the chocolate sauce: Put the chocolate in a microwave-safe bowl and microwave on high for 2½ to 3 minutes, or until softened and shiny. The chocolate will not melt completely. Add the cream and coffee and stir until smooth. Set aside at room temperature.

4. Heat two 9-inch nonstick pans over low heat. If you have seasoned 9-inch crepe pans, use them. Spray lightly with vegetable oil spray and ladle 3 tablespoons of crepe batter into the pans. Tip and roll the pans to spread the batter evenly over the bottom of the pans and cook for about 2 minutes. Using a spatula, flip the crepes and cook for 2 minutes longer, or until lightly browned. Lift the crepes from the pans and stack on a plate. These crepes do not stick to one another. Continue cooking the crepes until you have 16. Expect to throw out the first crepe in each pan; this is typical, as anyone who has made crepes knows. The first one never works, and after it has flopped, the pan is seasoned appropriately so that the rest are perfect.

5. Open the cans of boiled condensed milk. The milk will be caramel brown and thick.

6. Lay the crepes on a work surface. Spread a thick stripe—about 2 tablespoons—of *dulce de leche* (the boiled condensed milk) down the center of each crepe. Top the *dulce de leche* with an equal-sized stripe of whipped cream. Roll the crepes like a cigar and put 2 crepes on each plate.

7. Ladle about 3 tablespoons of chocolate sauce over the crepes and serve with the ice cream.

Flan

Our flan recipe comes from an unlikely place: a steelhead fishing lodge in northern British Columbia. We went through dozens of versions of flan over the years before we arrived at one that was good enough for Sasa or easy enough to replicate day in and day out. One October, Andy was having dinner at a remote lodge in the freezing British Columbian north woods when the proprietor's wife, Lola Britton, a native of Mexico, served this flan. The flavor was perfect, the texture was perfect—and she was a sweetheart and gave him the recipe.

There are a few tricks to ensure the best results. First, don't be afraid to burn the sugar—you want it dark, and you can always throw it away and start again if it goes too far. Second, invest in tall flan cups that you can find at specialty cooking stores. Last, take the flan out of the oven when the top starts to stick to your fingers and feels just solid. It will continue to cook outside the oven.

Serves 9

2 cups sugar	One 14-ounce can condensed milk	1 cup whole milk
1 cup water	8 large egg yolks	One 12-ounce can evaporated milk

1. Preheat the oven to 325°F. Position a rack in the center of the oven.

2. In a saucepan, heat the sugar in ½ cup of the water over medium heat. Cook for 8 to 11 minutes, stirring only once or twice, or until the thin sugar syrup is golden brown. Remove from the heat and stir in the remaining ½ cup water. Return to the heat and cook for about 4 minutes longer, or until the sugar dissolves and is the consistency of maple syrup. Cool for about 10 minutes.

3. Meanwhile, in the bowl of an electric mixer fitted with the whisk attachment and set on low speed, mix the condensed milk and egg yolks until combined. Add the whole milk and evaporated milk and beat for 2 to 3 minutes longer, or until the custard is thoroughly mixed. Do not overbeat, or bubbles will form. If they do, let them subside before continuing.

4. Put nine 8-ounce ramekins or flan cups in a roasting pan. Pour about 2 tablespoons of the caramelized sugar into each one and then top with about ½ cup of the custard. Put the pan on the oven rack and pour hot water into the pan to come halfway up the sides of the ramekins. Loosely cover with aluminum foil. Bake for about 1 hour, or until the custard jiggles in the center when shaken and sticks to your fingertips when touched gently.

5. Remove the ramekins from the roasting pan and let them cool.

6. Run a dull kitchen knife around the sides of each ramekin. Invert the ramekins onto each of 9 plates and lift them off the custard. The caramel sauce in the bottom of the ramekins will drip down the sides of the flans. Serve immediately.

Pineapple Upside-Down Cake

Slice-and-serve cakes such as this one are great for entertaining. Lisa Varnberg, executive chef in Greenwich, came up with the recipe when she saw a lot of extra pineapples in the cooler one day. She adapted it from a recipe developed by Chicago pastry chef Gale Gand, adding lemon juice to the cake batter to balance the flavor of the caramelized pineapple. It's a flexible dessert and does well when made with mangoes, apples, or peaches. If you don't have a cast-iron skillet, caramelize the fruit in a heavy pan and transfer it to a baking dish. When you work with hot sugar, as in step 2, it's a good idea to keep a small bowl of ice water nearby so if you get burned you can immediately submerge your finger or wrist in the water.

Serves 8

Pineapple

6 tablespoons unsalted butter

¾ cup packed dark brown sugar

½ medium pineapple, peeled, cored, quartered, and sliced ¼ inch thick

Cake Batter

1¼ cups all-purpose flour

2 teaspoons baking powder

¼ teaspoon salt

Grated zest and juice of 2 large lemons (about 3 teaspoons zest and about ½ cup juice)

1½ cups sugar

6 tablespoons unsalted butter, softened

1 tablespoon dark rum

1 teaspoon pure vanilla extract

2 large eggs

1. Preheat the oven to 350°F.

2. To prepare the pineapple: In a 10-inch cast-iron skillet, melt the butter over medium-high heat. Add the brown sugar and cook, carefully stirring occasionally with a wooden spoon, for about 5 minutes, or until thickened.

3. Arrange the pineapple slices in overlapping rows on top of the sugar. If you prefer, arrange them in a circular pattern. Set aside at room temperature.

4. To make the cake batter: In a large mixing bowl, whisk together the flour, baking powder, salt, and lemon zest.

5. In the bowl of an electric mixer fitted with the whisk attachment and set on medium-high speed, beat the sugar and softened butter for 5 to 7 minutes, or until light and fluffy. Add the lemon juice, rum, and vanilla and beat for about 1 minute.

6. Add 1 egg, mix until incorporated, and then mix in half the flour mixture. Beat on low speed for 2 to 3 minutes. Add the remaining egg, beat until incorporated, and then add the rest of the flour and mix until incorporated.

7. Pour the batter over the pineapple and bake for about 45 minutes, or until a toothpick inserted in the center of the cake comes out clean. Let the cake sit in the pan for 5 to 10 minutes, during which time the sugar syrup will be absorbed by the cake. Put a serving plate over the top of the skillet, turn upside down and let the cake slide onto the plate. Serve warm.

Churros y Chocoláte

These are Spanish street food, served in paper cones at carnivals, and kids love them. We have nights when the fryer can't keep up with the steady stream of orders, so if you plan to make them for a large group, put them on a platter as you take them from the fryer and invite people to help themselves. There is just no way to mass-produce them.

After Chef Lisa Varnberg introduced these in Greenwich, we added them to all the menus, although the chefs protested. You can't cut corners when you make churros, which means you can't make them ahead of time. Our interpretation of churros may be a little different from those you have had in Spain, which tend to be a little drier and less cakey. We make ours the way we do so that the dough can be pushed through a pastry bag directly into the hot oil.

The hot chocolate is bittersweet or semisweet to offset the sugared churros. Jazzed up with hot pepper flakes and dark rum, it turns straight donuts into something special.

Serves 8

Churros

3 cups water

1 cup (2 sticks) unsalted butter

1½ teaspoons salt

4 cups all-purpose flour

11 large eggs, lightly beaten

¼ cup olive oil

8 cups vegetable oil

3 cups sugar

3 tablespoons ground cinnamon

Chocoláte

8 cups whole milk

¾ teaspoon hot red pepper flakes

½ cup cornstarch

2 cups heavy cream

28 ounces bittersweet or semisweet chocolate, coarsely chopped (about 3½ cups)

1 cup sugar

½ cup Dutch-process (alkalized) unsweetened cocoa powder

½ dark rum

4 cups sweetened whipped cream (about 2 cups heavy cream plus sugar to taste), for garnish

1. To prepare the churros batter: In a large pot, bring the water, butter, and salt to a boil over high heat and cook until the butter melts.

2. Whisk in the flour and stir with a wooden spoon for 7 to 9 minutes over medium heat until the batter is pastelike and stiff.

3. Transfer the paste to a bowl of an electric mixer fitted with the paddle attachment and set on medium-low speed. Add the eggs and olive oil and mix for about 6 minutes, or until thoroughly combined. Set aside to rest for at least 1 hour and up to 24 hours. If the batter will rest for longer than an hour, lay plastic wrap directly on its surface and refrigerate until needed.

4. To make the *chocoláte*: Set a large saucepan over medium-low heat and, when hot, pour the milk into the pan, add the red pepper flakes, and let the milk come to a low simmer.

5. In a large glass measuring cup or similar container, stir the cornstarch into the cream and then pour into the simmering milk. Raise the heat to medium and stir constantly for 7 to 10 minutes, or until thickened.

6. Put the chocolate, sugar, and cocoa in a large bowl and strain the thickened milk mixture through a fine-mesh sieve over the chocolate. Let stand for about 10 minutes and then whisk well until smooth and thick. Stir in the rum.

7. Lay plastic wrap directly on top of the *chocoláte* and set aside until needed. (If not using right away, cool and refrigerate for up to 2 days. Reheat in the microwave for about 2 minutes on high.)

8. To fry the churros: Heat a deep, heavy pot over medium-low heat and, when hot, pour in the vegetable oil. Let it heat to 350°F on a deep-fat thermometer, or until the oil bubbles when a cube of bread is dropped in it and the bread moves slightly in the oil.

9. Meanwhile, in a large, wide mixing bowl, whisk together the sugar with the cinnamon and set aside.

10. Scoop the batter for the churros into a piping bag fitted with a wide, fluted tip and very carefully pipe 6-inch lengths of batter directly into the hot oil. This might require a little strength as the dough is thick. Fry for 5 to 8 minutes, or until the churros are crisp, lightly browned, and puffed. Turn at least once to ensure even browning.

11. With a slotted spoon, remove the churros from the oil, drain briefly, and, while still hot, toss with the cinnamon sugar. Transfer the sugared churros to a wax paper–lined jelly-roll pan or baking sheet and serve warm. Keep frying churros until you have 32, or 4 per serving.

12. Spoon about a cup of the warmed *chocoláte* into 8 small mugs or coffee cups. Top each with about 2 tablespoons of whipped cream. Serve the churros alongside the chocolate for dipping.

Bread Pudding with Roasted Summer Peaches and Dulce de Leche

One of our chefs, Lisa Varnberg, entered the walk-in at the West Hartford restaurant one day only to see a few trays of leftover brioche rolls along with a flat of *very* ripe peaches. Being mindful of food costs (as all our chefs must be), she came up with this bread pudding. Whenever this bread pudding goes on the menu, it sells out.

Serves 8

One 12-ounce can condensed milk

6 ripe peaches or nectarines, halved, pitted, and cut into sixths

12 large eggs

4 cups heavy cream

2 cups sugar

¾ cup peach schnapps

2 tablespoons unsalted butter

8 to 10 cups 1-inch cubes egg bread, such as challah or brioche (1 loaf challah or 2 loaves brioche)

1. Remove the label from the can of condensed milk and submerge it in a large pot filled with water. Bring to a boil over high heat, reduce to a rapid simmer, and simmer for about 3 hours. Add water as needed to cover the can by at least 1 inch. Check often to make sure the can is always covered with water; otherwise it could explode. Remove the can from the water and let it cool.

2. Preheat the oven to 425°F.

3. Spread the peaches in the pan and roast for 15 to 20 minutes, or until the fruit is soft and slightly browned. Turn off the oven.

4. Meanwhile, in a large mixing bowl, whisk together the eggs, cream, sugar, and schnapps.

5. Butter a 9 by 11-inch baking pan. Spread the bread in the pan, pour the egg batter over the bread, and mix well, mashing and squeezing the bread cubes with your hands. Refrigerate and let the bread absorb the liquid for at least 45 minutes and up to 4 hours. (The longer you let the bread pudding rest, the better it will be. If you know you will be able to let it rest for several hours, you don't have to mash and squeeze it quite as much.)

6. Remove from the refrigerator and add the fruit to the bread pudding. Stir gently to distribute it evenly.

7. Preheat the oven to 325°F.

8. Open the can of condensed milk. The milk will be caramel brown and thick. Using a tablespoon, dot the pudding with the *dulce de leche* (the boiled condensed milk) and gently push it into the pudding. Cover the pan with aluminum foil and bake for about 1½ hours, or until the custard sets.

9. Remove the foil and let the pudding cool for about 30 minutes. Spoon into bowls and serve warm or at room temperature.

Seasonal Brandied Fruits

Although you won't find this dessert on our restaurant menus, it shows up at our catered parties all the time. It holds up well when made ahead. In fact, it's best to allow the fruit ample time to macerate in the brandy because it just gets better. It's not for kids but is perfect for grown-ups who like to cook with the seasons. We have provided four variations, one for each season, so you can use the best and freshest ingredients available at a particular time of year.

Serves 4 to 6

1 pint vanilla ice cream, for serving

fall

2 Honey Crisp apples, or similar crisp and sweet apples, peeled and cored

2 firm, ripe pears, such as Bosc or Anjou, peeled and cored

1 pint strawberries, hulled and quartered

1 pint blueberries

1 cup VSOP brandy or other high-quality Armagnac or cognac

½ cup turbinado sugar, such as Sugar in the Raw

2 teaspoons chopped fresh mint leaves

winter

1 ripe mango, peeled and pitted

1 small papaya, peeled and seeded

½ ripe pineapple, peeled and cored

1 pint raspberries

⅓ cup turbinado sugar, such as Sugar in the Raw

1 cup VSOP brandy or other high-quality Armagnac or cognac

2 tablespoons chopped peeled fresh ginger

spring

1 pound sweet pitted cherries

1 pint strawberries, hulled and quartered

1 pint blackberries

1 cup VSOP brandy or other high-quality Armagnac or cognac

½ cup turbinado sugar, such as Sugar in the Raw

2 teaspoons chopped fresh mint leaves or lemon balm

summer

3 plums, pitted, or ½ ripe melon (such as cantaloupe or honeydew), peeled and seeded

2 peaches or nectarines, pitted

1 pint raspberries

1 cup VSOP brandy or other high-quality Armagnac or cognac

⅓ cup turbinado sugar, such as Sugar in the Raw

1 tablespoon chopped fresh basil, lemon thyme, or mint leaves

1. Dice the fruit into ½-inch pieces. Do not dice the berries.

2. In a mixing bowl, gently toss the diced fruit and berries with the brandy, sugar, and herbs (or the ginger if mixing winter fruits). Take care not to crush the fruit.

3. Spoon the ice cream into serving bowls and top with the fruit. Drizzle any collected juice from the bowl over both and serve.

Bananas Foster

This nonflammable version of the famous New Orleans dessert is extremely home-cook friendly. It's a good dessert to make ahead and can be reheated in the microwave for two or three minutes. It's a good way to use up overripe bananas, although it works equally well with less ripe fruit. We serve it with ice cream, but it pairs well, too, with pound cake.

Serves 8

¾ cup packed dark brown sugar

4 tablespoons unsalted butter

½ cup freshly squeezed orange juice

¼ cup dark rum

8 ripe bananas, peeled and sliced lengthwise

2 pints vanilla ice cream, for serving

1. In a 10-inch cast-iron skillet, heat the sugar and butter over medium-high heat and simmer, stirring occasionally with a wooden spoon, for 5 to 7 minutes, or until thickened. Stir in the orange juice and rum.

2. Lay as many bananas as will fit comfortably in the pan, cut sides down, and sauté for about 5 minutes, or until lightly browned and softened. As they are done, carefully lift the bananas from the pan and put 2 on each serving plate. Add the remaining bananas to the pan and cook them.

3. Spoon the pan sauce over the bananas and serve with ice cream.

Poached Pears

Spaniards love poached pears, and with good reason. When she was last in Barcelona, Lisa Varnberg, our Greenwich chef, ordered them at Aback, a two-star Michelin restaurant, where they were presented rolled in spice cake crumbs and decorated with a crispy tuile. These are not as dressy but are just as delicious. For more decorative pears, leave thin strips of skin on the pears when you peel them.

Serves 8

4 cups dry red wine

1½ cups sugar

1 cup brandy

8 or 9 black peppercorns

2 star anise

4 cloves

One 3-inch cinnamon stick

8 firm, ripe pears, such as Anjou or Bartlett, peeled and cored

1. In a deep saucepan, heat the wine, sugar, brandy, and spices over medium heat until simmering. Simmer for 12 to 15 minutes to give the flavors time to develop.

2. Submerge the pears in the poaching liquid. Lay a plate on top of the pears to keep them covered with liquid.

3. Reduce the heat to medium-low and poach for 18 to 20 minutes, or until tender. Using a slotted spoon, remove the pears and transfer 1 pear to each of 8 serving plates. Set aside in a warm area of the kitchen.

4. Raise the heat to high and bring the liquid to a boil. Boil for 20 to 25 minutes, or until the liquid reduces by about three-quarters and reaches a saucelike consistency.

5. Strain the sauce through a fine-mesh sieve. Spoon the sauce around the pears and serve.

Arroz con Leche

This is a classic Spanish "mother's dessert" utilizing yesterday's leftover rice. In Spain, it's found in the loftiest restaurant as well as every modest home kitchen. In the fancy restaurants, the chef might dress it up with foam or another garnish or add a variety of dried fruit. In northern Spain you are apt to find dried cherries in the rice pudding, whereas dried apricots are common in Mallorca. When we serve it, we like to make it very adult with a drizzling of sweet, syrupy Pedro Ximénez sherry. Although we suggest you cook the rice for the pudding, use any unseasoned leftover medium- or long-grain rice.

Serves 8

3¾ cups water

1¼ cups white medium- or long-grain rice

6 cups whole milk

6 tablespoons unsalted butter

2½ cups sugar

5 large eggs, beaten

3 tablespoons brandy

2 teaspoons pure vanilla extract

1 teaspoon grated orange zest

¼ teaspoon salt

½ cup golden raisins

1. Preheat the oven to 350°F. Position a rack in the center of the oven.

2. In a medium saucepan, bring the water to a boil over high heat. Add the rice, stir once or twice, reduce the heat to medium-low, cover, and cook for about 20 minutes, or until all the water is absorbed. Let the rice cool slightly. You can cook the rice ahead of time and let it cool completely.

3. In a saucepan, heat the milk, cooked rice, and butter over medium heat until simmering gently. Cook for 7 to 10 minutes, stirring occasionally, until the butter melts and the rice absorbs some of the milk. Adjust the heat to maintain the simmer. The milk will simmer, but do not let it boil. When the mixture is cooked, let it cool slightly, until you can touch it without burning your finger.

4. In a mixing bowl, whisk together the sugar, eggs, brandy, vanilla, orange zest, and salt. Pour the rice and milk into the bowl and stir well. Fold in the raisins.

5. Transfer the rice mixture to an 8-inch-square pan and set the pan in a larger roasting pan. Put the roasting pan on the oven's center rack and pour hot water into the larger pan so that it comes halfway up the sides of the smaller pan.

6. Bake for about 1 hour, or until the pudding is set and slightly thickened but still fluid. Let the pudding cool in the pan still set in the water bath for 45 minutes.

7. Spoon into 8 serving bowls and serve.

Profiteroles with Ice Cream and Chocolate Sauce

If you want to go all out, this is a spectacular-looking dessert. Making the choux paste—cream puff batter—is somewhat advanced baking, but the rest of the dessert is easy. The assembly is where the artist in you emerges. For a group, try building an enormous pyramid of profiteroles and taking it to the table for people to attack.

Serves 8

1 cup water

½ cup (1 stick) unsalted butter

¼ teaspoon salt

1 cup all-purpose flour

1 teaspoon baking powder

3 large eggs

2 pints vanilla or your favorite flavor ice cream

Chocolate Sauce (page 180)

1. Preheat the oven to 350°F.

2. In a medium saucepan, bring the water, butter, and salt to a boil over high heat and cook until the butter melts. Reduce the heat to medium and, using a wooden spoon, stir in the flour and baking powder to make a paste. Cook for 6 to 8 minutes, stirring, or until a film forms on the bottom of the pan.

3. In the bowl of an electric mixer fitted with the paddle attachment and set on medium speed, beat the hot paste with 1 egg for 2 to 3 minutes, or until the egg is incorporated. Add the other 2 eggs, 1 at a time, beating well after each addition. Cover with plastic wrap and refrigerate for at least 1 hour and up to 24 hours to chill.

4. Preheat the oven to 400°F. Line 2 jelly-roll pans with parchment paper.

5. Spoon golf ball–sized rounds of batter onto the parchment paper. You should have 24 rounds. Or fit a pastry bag with a wide, no fluted tip and form 24 rounds.

6. Bake the rounds for 10 minutes, rotate the pans, lower the oven temperature to 350°F, and cook for about 25 minutes longer, or until the rounds are browned and crisp. Remove from the oven and set aside to cool for 15 to 20 minutes.

7. Slice each puff in half and put 3 bottom halves on each of 8 serving plates. Put a small scoop of ice cream on top of each half and replace the 3 top halves, creating mini-sandwiches. Drizzle each plate with about 2 tablespoons of chocolate sauce and serve.

Orange and Almond Cake

This is the classic *torte de Santiago* made in Galicia, the region of northwestern Spain to the north of Portugal that faces the Atlantic Ocean. At certain times of year Spanish home cooks make this cake topped with a cross (created with confectioners' sugar and a paper template) to honor Saint James. We also dust the cake with confectioners' sugar before serving. A few years ago we held a harvest wine dinner, and this was selected as the dessert course. It was perfect with the autumn flavors and the wines. It's very easy to make and can also be baked as a sheet cake, topped with sliced apples. Try this served with melted vanilla ice cream as a sauce—a cheater's crème anglaise.

Serves 8

1 cup sugar

7 large eggs, separated

½ teaspoon grated orange zest

½ pound roasted whole almonds

¼ teaspoon orange flower oil

5 Granny Smith apples, peeled, cored, and quartered

1 to 2 tablespoons honey, if needed

Confectioners' sugar, for serving

1. In the bowl of an electric mixer fitted with the whisk attachment and set on medium-high speed, cream the sugar, egg yolks, and orange zest for about 6 minutes, or until pale and fluffy.

2. In a food processor fitted with the metal blade, grind the almonds until finely ground to the consistency of granulated sugar. Fold the ground nuts into the batter. Stir in the orange oil.

3. In the clean, dry bowl of an electric mixer fitted with the whisk attachment and set on high speed, beat the egg whites for 5 to 7 minutes, or until stiff peaks form.

4. Preheat the oven to 350°F. Butter two 8-inch round cake pans.

5. Using a rubber spatula, fold about a quarter of the beaten egg whites into the batter to lighten it. Gently fold in the rest of the egg whites.

6. Divide the batter between the pans and bake for about 45 minutes, or until a toothpick inserted in the center of the cakes comes out clean. Let the cake layers cool in the pans set on wire racks. Do not turn off the oven.

7. Spread the apples in a shallow roasting pan and roast for about 15 minutes, or until the apples soften and brown slightly. Transfer the apples to a bowl and, using a potato masher, mash them until coarsely, leaving some chunks. If the apples are tart, you may want to add the honey. If they are sweet, you may not need it.

8. Invert a cake layer on a serving plate and spread the apple mash over it. Top with the second layer and dust with confectioners' sugar.

Barcelona Fruit Crisp

This dessert is nearly always on the menu and is a great way to use fruit that is starting to soften. We change the filling with the season, using apples and pears in the fall and relying on stone fruits such as peaches and plums in the summer. Pineapple, mango, and berries are also delicious.

The crisp is a forgiving recipe, which means you can double or halve it very easily. Any leftover filling can be used to fill crepes or to add flavor and color to bread pudding.

Serves 8

Topping

1 cup all-purpose flour

1 cup packed dark brown sugar

1 cup rolled oats

1 cup (2 sticks) unsalted butter, chilled

½ teaspoon salt

Fruit Filling

4 Granny Smith or other firm, tart apples, peeled, cored, and chopped into 1-inch dice

4 firm ripe pears, such as Bosc or Anjou, peeled, cored, and chopped into 1-inch dice

½ cup granulated sugar

¼ cup freshly squeezed lemon juice

2 tablespoons cornstarch

2 pints vanilla ice cream, for serving

1. To make the topping: Preheat the oven to 350°F. Line a jelly roll pan with parchment paper.

2. In a food processor fitted with the metal blade, pulse the flour, dark brown sugar, oats, butter, and salt until the mixture resembles peas.

3. Spread the topping over the parchment paper and bake for 35 to 40 minutes, stirring frequently, until crisp and honey brown. Cool the topping in the pan set on a wire rack.

4. To make the fruit filling: In a large saucepan, cook the fruit and granulated sugar over medium-low heat and simmer for 15 to 20 minutes, or until the fruit releases its juice. Raise the heat to medium-high and bring the fruit and juices to a gentle boil.

5. Meanwhile, in a small bowl, stir together the lemon juice and cornstarch. Pour into the saucepan and boil for 2 to 3 minutes, or until the juices run clear and the mixture thickens.

6. Spoon the fruit into each of 8 serving bowls. Top generously with the crisp mixture and serve immediately with ice cream.

summer fruit variation: In place of the apples and pears, substitute:

1 ripe pineapple, peeled, cored, and chopped into 1-inch dice

1 ripe mango; peeled, pit removed, and chopped into 1-inch dice

1 pint strawberries, hulled and halved, or ½ pint blueberries

sources for spanish ingredients and foods

Amigofoods.com
350 NE 75th Street
Miami, Florida 33138
800-627-2544
www.amigofoods.com

Delicias de España
4016 SW 57th Avenue
Miami, Florida 33155
305-669-4485
www.deliciasdeespana.com

La Tienda
3601 La Grange Parkway
Toano, Virginia 23168
800-710-4304
www.tienda.com

Marky's
687 NE 79th Street
Miami, Florida 33138
800-522-8427
www.markys.com

Sabor of Spain
1303 4th Street
San Rafael, California 94901
415-457-8466
www.saborofspain.com

**The Spanish Table
(4 locations)**
www.spanishtable.com

The Spanish Table
1426 Western Avenue
Seattle, Washington 98101
206-682-2827
seattle@spanishtable.com

The Spanish Table 2
1814 San Pablo Avenue
Berkeley, California 94702
510-548-1383
berkeley@spanishtable.com

The Spanish Table 3
109 N Guadalupe Street
Santa Fe, New Mexico 87501
505-986-0243
santafe@spanishtable.com

The Spanish Table 4
800 Redwood Highway 123
Mill Valley, California 94941
415-388-5043
millvalley@spanishtable.com

**Whole Foods
(various locations
throughout the United
States, Canada, and
the United Kingdom)**
www.wholefoodsmarket.com

Zingerman's
422 Detroit Street
Ann Arbor, Michigan 48104
888-636-8162
www.zingermans.com

metric conversions and equivalents

metric conversion formulas

to convert	multiply
Ounces to grams	Ounces by 28.35
Pounds to kilograms	Pounds by .454
Teaspoons to milliliters	Teaspoons by 4.93
Tablespoons to milliliters	Tablespoons by 14.79
Fluid ounces to milliliters	Fluid ounces by 29.57
Cups to milliliters	Cups by 236.59
Cups to liters	Cups by .236
Pints to liters	Pints by .473
Quarts to liters	Quarts by .946
Gallons to liters	Gallons by 3.785
Inches to centimeters	Inches by 2.54

approximate metric equivalents

volume

$\frac{1}{4}$ teaspoon	1 milliliter
$\frac{1}{2}$ teaspoon	2.5 milliliters
$\frac{3}{4}$ teaspoon	4 milliliters
1 teaspoon	5 milliliters
$1\frac{1}{4}$ teaspoon	6 milliliters
$1\frac{1}{2}$ teaspoon	7.5 milliliters
$1\frac{3}{4}$ teaspoon	8.5 milliliters
2 teaspoons	10 milliliters
1 tablespoon ($\frac{1}{2}$ fluid ounce)	15 milliliters
2 tablespoons (1 fluid ounce)	30 milliliters
$\frac{1}{4}$ cup	60 milliliters
$\frac{1}{3}$ cup	80 milliliters
$\frac{1}{2}$ cup (4 fluid ounces)	120 milliliters
$\frac{2}{3}$ cup	160 milliliters
$\frac{3}{4}$ cup	180 milliliters
1 cup (8 fluid ounces)	240 milliliters
$1\frac{1}{4}$ cups	300 milliliters
$1\frac{1}{2}$ cups (12 fluid ounces)	360 milliliters
$1\frac{2}{3}$ cups	400 milliliters
2 cups (1 pint)	460 milliliters
3 cups	700 milliliters
4 cups (1 quart)	0.95 liter
1 quart plus $\frac{1}{4}$ cup	1 liter
4 quarts (1 gallon)	3.8 liters

weight

$\frac{1}{4}$ ounce	7 grams
$\frac{1}{2}$ ounce	14 grams
$\frac{3}{4}$ ounce	21 grams
1 ounce	28 grams
$1\frac{1}{4}$ ounces	35 grams
$1\frac{1}{2}$ ounces	42.5 grams
$1\frac{2}{3}$ ounces	45 grams
2 ounces	57 grams
3 ounces	85 grams
4 ounces ($\frac{1}{4}$ pound)	113 grams
5 ounces	142 grams
6 ounces	170 grams
7 ounces	198 grams
8 ounces ($\frac{1}{2}$ pound)	227 grams
16 ounces (1 pound)	454 grams
35.25 ounces (2.2 pounds)	1 kilogram

length

$\frac{1}{8}$ inch	3 millimeters
$\frac{1}{4}$ inch	6 millimeters
$\frac{1}{2}$ inch	$1\frac{1}{4}$ centimeters
1 inch	$2\frac{1}{2}$ centimeters
2 inches	5 centimeters
$2\frac{1}{2}$ inches	6 centimeters
4 inches	10 centimeters
5 inches	13 centimeters
6 inches	$15\frac{1}{4}$ centimeters
12 inches (1 foot)	30 centimeters

oven temperatures

To convert Fahrenheit to Celsius, subtract 32 from Fahrenheit, multiply the result by 5, then divide by 9.

description	fahrenheit	celsius	british gas mark
Very cool	200°	95°	0
Very cool	225°	110°	$\frac{1}{4}$
Very cool	250°	120°	$\frac{1}{2}$
Cool	275°	135°	1
Cool	300°	150°	2
Warm	325°	165°	3
Moderate	350°	175°	4
Moderately hot	375°	190°	5
Fairly hot	400°	200°	6
Hot	425°	220°	7
Very hot	450°	230°	8
Very hot	475°	245°	9

common ingredients and their approximate equivalents

1 cup uncooked white rice = 185 grams

1 cup all-purpose flour = 140 grams

1 stick butter (4 ounces • $\frac{1}{2}$ cup • 8 tablespoons) = 110 grams

1 cup butter (8 ounces • 2 sticks • 16 tablespoons) = 220 grams

1 cup brown sugar, firmly packed = 225 grams

1 cup granulated sugar = 200 grams

Information compiled from a variety of sources, including *Recipes into Type* by Joan Whitman and Dolores Simon (Newton, MA: Biscuit Books, 2000); *The New Food Lover's Companion* by Sharon Tyler Herbst (Hauppauge, NY: Barron's, 1995); and *Rosemary Brown's Big Kitchen Instruction Book* (Kansas City, MO: Andrews McMeel, 1998).

index